An old Punjaubee

The Punjaub and North-West Frontier of India

An old Punjaubee

The Punjaub and North-West Frontier of India

ISBN/EAN: 9783337145330

Printed in Europe, USA, Canada, Australia, Japan

Cover: Foto ©Andreas Hilbeck / pixelio.de

More available books at **www.hansebooks.com**

THE PUNJAUB

AND

NORTH-WEST FRONTIER OF INDIA.

BY

AN OLD PUNJAUBEE.

LONDON:
C. KEGAN PAUL & CO., 1 PATERNOSTER SQUARE.
1878.

PREFACE.

THE following pages have been written with the object of presenting a rough sketch of a country and people destined to play an important part in the not very distant future, as some of us think.

I can hardly hope to *amuse* English readers with descriptions of countries and races so little known to them, but if I can only induce them to take some interest in a subject which is acquiring greater importance with every fresh move of Russian diplomacy, I shall be content. The authorities I have consulted are Cunningham's 'History of the Sikhs,' Blue Books, official reports and papers; and for much connected with the frontier tribes I have relied on personal observation extending over ten or twelve years. There are two excellent works on the latter subject, Sir R. Temple's 'Notice of the Frontier Tribes,' and Colonel

PREFACE.

Paget's 'History of the Punjaub Irregular Force,' but I have not had the opportunity of consulting either, nor are they accessible to the general public. I have avoided Oriental terms as far as possible, but have been obliged, of course, to call the representatives of the tribes by their right names.

CONTENTS.

Part I.

CHAPTER I.

Geographical description of the Punjaub—The rivers—The Bár or waste—Its inhabitants—The 'Khój' or tracking system—Classification of the population by creeds—The Hindoos — The Mohammedans 1

CHAPTER II.

Brief History of the Sikhs—Decrease in their numbers—Religion—The 'Kooka' schismatics—Causes which led to the war with the British in 1845-46—Claimants to the throne after Runjeet Singh's death—The 'Jumoo' Rajahs—The army—Punchayuts—Sikh army crosses the Sutlej—Battles that followed—Final victory of the British at Sobrâon 11

CHAPTER III.

Administration of the Punjaub under a British Resident—Intrigues against the British by the Rânee—Siege of Mooltan—Battles of Ramnuggur and Chiliânwâla—Final victory at Goojerât and annexation of the Punjaub. 26

CHAPTER IV.

Geographical description of North-West frontier—The Affghans—Their political relations—The 'Jirgahs'—Comparison of the Affghans with the Americans of Cortes's time—Affghan independence of Câbul—Description of the Pathân tribes—The 'Chigurzye'—'Hussunzye'—The Mudah Khail and Amayze—The 'Judoons'—Bonairs—Swâtees—Momunds—Bâjourees . 36

CHAPTER V.

Causes which led to the Umbelah campaign—The Hindostanee fanatics—Assemblage of the British force—Military and political difficulties—Occupation of Umbelah Pass by our troops—Constant state of warfare for two months—Final victory at 'Lâloo'—Lessons to be derived from this campaign—Notice of the 'Akhoond' of Swât 47

CHAPTER VI.

The 'Bonairs'—Their fighting strength—The 'Momunds'—Their hostility to us—'The 'Afreedees'—The 'Kohât' Pass—The 'Khutuks'—The 'Wuzeerees'—The 'Câbul Khail'—The 'Oomurzye'—Expeditions against those tribes—The 'Muhsoods'—Description of their country—Attack on our frontier by a large body of the tribe 62

CHAPTER VII.

Campaign against the Muhsoods—Its results—The Butunnees—Sheoranees—Oosterânees—The Powindah merchants—The Bilooch tribes—Their character as compared with the Pathâns—The Scinde frontier—The Punjaub frontier force . . 74

CONTENTS.

Part II.

CHAPTER VIII.

Characteristics of the border tribes—Their religion—Blood-feuds—Theft—Treatment of women—Social customs—Hypothesis of the Affghâns being the lost Ten Tribes of Israel—The 'Vesh'—Similarity of this custom to Jewish institutions—Arms of the Affghans—Military system—Treachery of the Affghans—Strength of the different tribes 91

CHAPTER IX.

Systems of frontier management—In Scinde—In the Punjaub—Duties of the Lieutenant-Governor in connection with it—Pressure of work—Proposed change in system—Advantages thereof—Policy of conciliation so called—Not successful—Failure of Sir Lewis Pelly's mission—Detail of staff for Border Commissioner 105

CHAPTER X.

Method of dealing with the frontier tribes—Policy of prompt chastisement not properly carried out—Causes of the same—Character of various expeditions against the tribes—That against the Jowâkees—Means available for carrying out expeditions . 120

CHAPTER XI.

Political dealings with Câbul—Hostility of the Affghans during the 'Sikh' war of 1848-49—Change of feeling—Application of Ameer Dost Mahomed to the Governor-General—Subsidies of money and arms granted—Strife for the succession after Dost Mahomed's death—Final success of Sher Ali—His feelings towards us—His visit to Lord Mayo in 1869—Character of Sher Ali—The conciliation policy—Advantages of the move to Quettah—Lord Lawrence's opinion on the subject—Remarks thereon 128

CONTENTS.

CHAPTER XII.

General remarks on the feelings of the natives of India towards the English—The Mohammedans—Opinions regarding them—Sir R. Temple—Vambéry—Sir G. Campbell—'Fraser's Magazine'—Major Osborn—Other opinions on this subject—State of feeling among Hindoos and others—Effects in India of rapid changes 142

CHAPTER XIII.

Relation of native soldiers with their officers—Of civil officers and ryots—Unsettled state of feeling in India—Social relations between Europeans and natives—Importance of union among English in India—Present want of *esprit de corps*—Russian movements in Central Asia, and their effect in India . . 156

CHAPTER XIV.

Further remarks on Russian movements in Central Asia—State of feeling among certain native chiefs in India—The native press of India — Reforms required in taxation — Police — Law—Army—Responsibilities of England to India—Conclusion . 170

THE PUNJAUB

AND

NORTH-WEST FRONTIER OF INDIA.

Part I.

CHAPTER I.

Geographical description of the Punjaub—The rivers—The Bâr or waste—Its inhabitants—The 'Khôj' or tracking system—Classification of the population by creeds—The Hindoos—The Mohammedans.

THE land of the Five Rivers or Punjaub proper is included in the tract between the 'Sutlej' and 'Indus' rivers, between which flow also the 'Béâs,' the 'Râvee,' the 'Chenaub,' and the 'Jhelum;' the deltas between the rivers being named after the respective rivers which bound them, by combining the initial letters or syllables of each river. Thus the delta between the Béâs and the Râvee is called the 'Bâ Ree' 'Dooâb' (land of two rivers); that between the Râvee and the Chenaub, the 'Re Chnâb;' and that between the Chenaub and the Jhelum, the 'Chu. J.' The delta between the Jhelum and the Indus rivers deviates from the above nomenclature, and is called the 'Sind-Sâgor' Dooâb, 'Sind' being the local name for the Indus.

But beyond the Punjaub proper a large tract to the south of the 'Sutlej' river, including the Ferozepore, Loodianah, and Umballa districts, has always been considered to form part of the Province, and later on, for convenience of local administration, after the Mutiny the Delhi and Hissâr divisions, which had formed part of the territory under the Agra Government, were added to the Punjaub; while to the north-west, the tract of country lying between the Indus and the Affghan mountains had been occupied by the 'Sikhs' under Runjeet Singh, and it was included as part of the British province of the Punjaub at the annexation of the country in 1849. The northern and western boundaries of the province are formed by the mountain ranges of the Himalayas, from Simla on the north-east to the Suleimani range, whose spurs reach the Scinde frontier to the westward. The 28th degree of north latitude represents nearly the southern, and the 78th degree of east longitude the eastern boundary.

Between the several rivers a large barren waste is found, the cultivation being confined to belts on each bank, varying more or less in extent. This waste is termed the 'Bâr,' and runs down the centre of each 'Dooâb' or delta, varying from forty or fifty miles in breadth at the base, to a mile or two as it approaches the apex formed by the junction of the rivers. In the early time of our occupation, these wastes owing to sparseness of population, remoteness from river irrigation, and the great depth at which water was found, were left almost entirely to the nomade breeders of camels, cattle, &c., plenty of fodder being found for the former in the small trees and prickly shrubs with which the waste abounded, and in a favourable rainy season grass in abundance was produced for the cattle. These secluded regions furnished also a safe refuge for cattle-stealers during the earlier period of our rule. Nothing was easier than to pounce upon an outlying herd belonging to the villages adjoining the 'Bâr' at night, and drive them off into the trackless wilderness, and by the time the luckless owners awoke to a sense of their loss, their cattle had been conveyed into the mazes of the jungle, where even with the assistance of the law recovery was well-nigh hopeless.

During the 'Sikh' dynasty, and for some time under our own more enlightened rule, no thorough effort was made to check this system of depredation, but civilisation has been attended here as everywhere else with its usual results. Increase of cultivation and growth of population, the handmaids of good government, are gradually reducing the limits of the waste, and, accompanied by a better system of police administration, we may look for their final victory in the complete suppression of these reivers of the wilderness.

The habits of these denizens of the waste were, as may be imagined, rude and uncouth to a degree. They lived chiefly on the produce of their herds; wheat or maize flour was a luxury, their bread being made principally of the seeds of a jungle grass pounded into flour. The taste was not unpleasant, but the gluten contained in the bread must have been represented by a very small decimal. In a plentiful rainy season water was obtained from ponds for the cattle and their owners, and under the same favourable circumstances grass was to be found in abundance; but, as a rule, the nomades generally constructed a well at each of their encampments. This was a work of difficulty and toil, as on the high ridge of the deltas water is not found at less than eighty or ninety feet, and sometimes much more, from the surface.

The process of well-making consisted in digging a shaft, often not more than four or five feet in diameter, and, as the excavation proceeded, lining the sides of the shaft with a kind of thick rope or fascine, constructed of twigs and coarse grass, to prevent the sides from falling in. With all their ingenuity, however, it not unfrequently happened that the earth gave way and inhumed the unfortunate excavator. The chief agency resorted to in former times, and which to a certain extent prevails still, for tracing stolen cattle in the 'Bâr' was the system called 'Khôj' or tracking. The trackers are professionals, and it was the practice to attach one of these adepts to Police Stations in certain localities. The English reader may acquire a fair idea of the process from Cooper's Indian novels. The ingenuity with which these men ravel out a track quite rivals the marvellous performances of 'Uncas' or 'Chingachgook,' and many a story is told of their perseverance in tracing animals through many miles of both waste and cultivation to a successful result. But the thieves are not without their ingenious contrivances to elude the 'Khôj.' The river is freely made use of where available; for, as 'Hawkeye' says—

'Running water leaves no trail.'

And when cattle are driven over the dry hard soil of the 'Bâr,' where the cloven hoof would betray its mark, the thieves shoe, or rather slipper, the animal with a leather bag tied round the fetlock, which effectually prevents the hoof from scratching the surface. The law of the 'Khôj' is, that on the 'Khoji' or tracker bringing the trace of stolen animals to a village, the headmen of the township are bound to show that the tracks proceed beyond their limits, or failing to produce the thief, to make good the value of the stolen cattle. This practice bears some analogy to the ordeal by which the Israelites were to free themselves from the charge of blood shed within the limits of their village (Deut. xxi. 1). The system has its drawbacks, the principal being that the right enforcement of it depends on the honesty of the tracker, a somewhat insecure foundation to build upon. It rests with him to declare whether the track has been brought home to a village or not, and it depends on the value and cogency of the arguments adduced by the villagers as to whether he can discover it on the other side, and so liberate them from responsibility.

The Punjaub occupies an area of 95,768 square miles, contains a population of 17,500,000, and is inhabited by peoples of widely differing characteristics as regards physique, habits, and religion.

The population,[1] classified by religions, consists of Sikhs, Hindoos, comprising several sections of that creed, Mohammedans of the Punjaub, Mohammedans of the frontier, and, in comparatively small numbers, Buddhists, who are found only in the hill regions. The Hindoos inhabiting the 'Punjaub' are, as noted above, of divers sects. The Brahmins here, as in Hindostan, hold the first place, and, the schismatic movement in Bengal not having yet reached the 'Punjaub,' reign supreme in all Hindoo communities. 'Rajpoots' are to be found principally among the tribes inhabiting the lower hills to the north-east, several of the petty Rajas of that quarter being of that tribe.

There are several other subdivisions of Hindoos, but none that call for special remark except the well-known and widely-spread race of 'Bunniahs' of the 'Khutrie' sect, and known commonly in the Punjaub by the appellation of 'Kirârs.' These small grain

[1] Details of Census of 1868:—

Males	9,581,292
Females	8,015,460
	17,596,752

Mohammedans	9,335,632
Hindoos	6,134,243
Sikhs	1,129,319
Europeans	17,938
Half-castes and native Christians	3,971
Other castes	972,833

Proportion of population to area:—

Punjaub	184	per square mile.
Bengal	311	,, ,,
North-West Provinces	420	,, ,,
Madras	170	,, ,,
Bombay	155	,, ,,

merchants, though their dealings are not confined to that commodity only, are to be found not only in the civilised parts of the Province, where life and property are tolerably secure, but also in the wildest parts of our frontier, both within and beyond the reach of British authority, in localities where one would suppose their lives and their earnings were not worth a moment's purchase. But still they live and thrive, and accumulate wealth like the Jewish usurer of old. Like them, perhaps, they are sometimes squeezed, and made to disgorge their gains; but, as a rule, they escape fire and torture, and live the life and die the death of the miser, their children following in their steps.

It is not to be understood that they always escape rough treatment, for it has not unfrequently happened on the frontier that a border 'Front de Bœuf' has seized a 'Bunniah,' and subjected him to much the same treatment as his Norman prototype proposed for Isaac the Jew until a suitable ransom was forthcoming.

Up to a not very remote date, a very large portion of the land paying revenue to Government was in the hands of this class by mortgage or purchase. During the turbulent period which intervened between the death of 'Runjeet Singh' and the inauguration of our rule, amid the constant struggles for the succession, great exactions were made upon the agricultural classes to replenish the empty exchequer and to furnish soldiers for the rival factions. The cultivation of the soil was consequently much neglected, and the tenants, improvident themselves, not being able to meet the requirements of the State on the one hand, and of their own domestic necessities and comforts on the other, and often not being able to provide seed for the periodical sowings, resorted to the Bunniahs, who lent them money on exorbitant terms on the security of their land, which was hypothecated to the Bunniahs, so that, as noted above, the greater portion of the land interest was in their hands; but as tranquillity increased under our rule, and as equitable assessments were made by our officers, in place of the old rack-renting process, the agriculturists began to recover themselves, and now the landholders in many parts of the country have freed themselves from their bonds, and form a wealthy and influential class. This, however, is by no means the universal condition, and the consequences of former misrule and improvidence still remain, while habits of comparative luxury, induced by greater prosperity and advancing civilisation, still conspire to keep the agricultural community more or less in the hands of the money-lending classes.

The Mohammedans of the Punjaub proper form the large majority of the population. In the census of 1868 they numbered 9,330,000 to 6,130,000 Hindoos and 1,130,000 Sikhs. This preponderance of Mohammedans over Hindoos is peculiar to the 'Punjaub.' Of the 200,000,000 in India, 160,000,000 are stated to be of the Hindoo persuasion, which gives a proportion of 4 to 1 in favour of the Hindoos generally.

It is natural perhaps that Mohammedanism should be in the ascendant in the Punjaub, from the fact of its having been the first part of India occupied by the

Mussulmans, and that on which they retained their hold even when driven out of Southern India.

The Mohammedan of the Punjaub does not differ much from his co-religionist of Hindostan, except that he is more regular in his devotions, and more scrupulous in the observance of the fasts and festivals of his creed. It would seem as if distance had something to do with religious sentiment, that is, that fervour is greatest at the point from whence the Mohammedan proselytisers issue, and becomes gradually diluted as leagues intervene. Thus the Mohammedan of Affghanistan and our frontier is far more fervid in his bigotry than the Mussulman of the Punjaub, and he again evinces more zeal for his creed than the Mohammedan of the plains of Hindostan. The latter, indeed, are often called by the orthodox Mussulmans of the North-West, 'Kâfir-i-Hind,' or Indian infidels. It will, of course, be understood that the above remark refers to the mass of the people, for it is certain that many of the higher class of Mohammedans in India are far better educated in the doctrine and principles of their creed than the semi-savage mountaineers of the Hindoo Koosh.

The Mohammedans of the Punjaub are, as a rule, a quiet and well-disposed race. They make good cultivators, and some of the officers of the Punjaub Irregular Force, which is largely recruited from their ranks, prefer them as soldiers to any other class. The Punjaub Mohammedans are almost universally of the 'Sûnni' persuasion. The number of converts or perverts to Mohammedanism in the Punjaub is considerable. Between the river 'Chenaub' and the

Indus, and in the southern portion of the Province, the population is chiefly of this class, but, as has been said above, the religious fervour of the Punjaubi Mussulmans not being excessive, they and their Hindoo brethren live contentedly side by side, and it frequently occurs that descendants from the same stock, and this among the Rajpoots especially, are to be found exercising joint authority in the village community, one representing the ancient Hindoo faith of their common forefather, the other the creed of the Mohammedan usurper.

In one instance, in the Mozuffergurh district, a Hindoo tribe, the 'Sigul,' a branch of the great 'Siâl' stock, were converted, the majority of them, to Mohammedanism, some three or four centuries ago, but to this day a Brahmin as well as a Moolah attends at the marriage ceremony of members of the tribe.

CHAPTER II.

Brief History of the Sikhs—Decrease in their numbers—Religion—The 'Kooka' schismatics—Causes which led to the war with the British in 1845-46—Claimants to the throne after Runjeet Singh's death—The 'Jumoo' Rajahs—The army—Punchayuts—Sikh army crosses the Sutlej—Battles that followed—Final victory of the British at Sobrâon.

THE Sikhs come next under consideration. Their history has been written by abler pens, and it does not fall within the scope of a brief sketch like this to enter at large upon the general history of the people.

Briefly, the Sikhs came into existence as a sect about A.D. 1510, Nanuk being the first prophet, and Gooroo Govind in 1700 the first religious leader. It is advisable to draw this distinction between the two principal apostles of 'Sikhism,' because the first was a peaceful schismatic from the Hindoo creed, while the latter supplemented the 'Gurunth'[1] with the sword. The power of the people culminated under Runjeet Singh (1798 to 1839), since when their decline, both in numbers and political power, has been manifest. One principal reason for this, apart from the obvious one that they are now a subject, instead of a governing race, is, that the religion is not, so to speak, hereditary.

[1] Gurunth, the 'Sikh' Holy Book.

The son of a 'Sikh' father is not necessarily a 'Sikh' himself. 'Fit, non nascitur.' He must be admitted by the solemn right of the 'Pahul,'[1] invested, as it were, with 'Sikh' attributes, before he can write himself 'Sikh' in fact; and it may be that, as the military power and glory of the sect has faded, there is less care on the part of the parents to perpetuate the race. 'The initiatory ceremony for adults is now rarely performed' (Punjaub Report for 1852-53). This diminution of the 'Sikhs' as a separate people was noticed so long ago as 1853, soon after the annexation of the Punjaub. In one of the early reports of the newly acquired Province, which was furnished in 1853, it is noted that 'the "Sikh" faith and ecclesiastical polity is rapidly going where the Sikh political ascendancy has already gone;' and again, in the report for 1854-55, 'The "Sikh" tribe is losing its numbers rapidly.'

It is not easy to arrive at a correct estimate of the numbers of the Sikh nation prior to our rule. Burnes in his 'Travels,' and Elphinstone, 'History of India,' estimate them at 500,000 souls. Cunningham, "History of the 'Sikhs,'" writing later, places the number at one and a quarter or one and a half millions; but these figures appear from subsequent local inquiry to have been below the mark. In 1854 it was assumed

---

[1] The ceremony of the 'Pahul' was as follows :—The novice, who must have reached the age of discrimination, stands with his hands joined in supplication and repeats after the priest the articles of his faith. Some sugar and water are stirred in a vessel with a double-edged dagger, and the water is sprinkled on his face and person; he drinks the remainder and exclaims "Wah Gooroo," which completes the ceremony. At least five Sikhs must be present at the ceremony, one being a priest. Women were sometimes, but not generally, initiated after the above formula.

that the Hindoo population of the Punjaub was five and a half millions, of which nearly one-half were supposed to be Sikhs; but in the census taken in January 1868, the Sikhs are returned as numbering only 1,130,000, to 6,130,000 of Hindoos. It was further ascertained in 1854 that in the Lahore and Umritsur divisions, in which is the 'Manjah' or original home of the Sikhs, there were only 200,000 in an aggregate population of 3,000,000. The figures exhibited in the census of 1868 are as nearly correct as any numbering of the peoples in India can hope to be; and assuming that the totals given in 1854 are approximate, the prophecy of the diminution of the 'Sikh' race may be considered as undergoing a rapid fulfilment.

This may be a fortunate circumstance for the stability of our rule in the Punjaub, for there can be little doubt that the 'Sikhs' were the most formidable enemies the British troops ever encountered in the field in India, and this too when they had lost the cohesion which made them so powerful under 'Runjeet Singh.'

The first 'Sikh' war with the British in 1845-46 followed on the numerous contests for the succession after 'Runjeet Singh's' death, during which period there was no leader of sufficient mark to keep in hand the conflicting agents in the strife for power, or to dominate with Runjeet Singh's stern will and iron hand the turbulent elements of which the 'Sikh' state was composed. Even with the disadvantages of incompetent and corrupt leaders, and divided counsels, we shall not readily forget the manner in which the 'Sikh' soldiers met us during the wars of 1845-46 and

1848-49. It is hardly too much to say, that if the 'Sikh' cavalry and reserve force under 'Tej Singh' had made good its advance at 'Feroz-Shuhur' on 22nd December 1845, after the deadly strife of the preceding day, when confusion and dismay reigned in our ranks, and when our leaders, Hardinge and Gough, thought that nothing remained but to die where they stood, we should have been driven back to Delhi. Thus the events of the Mutiny might have been anticipated by a decade, with this additional circumstance telling against us, that we should have had the 'Sikhs' in the ranks of our foes, instead of their being so powerful an element in our favour, as they proved.

The 'Sikh' religion does not recognise caste according to the 'Hindoo' view, though the people uphold the distinctions of race to a certain extent. The character of the people has been formed perhaps somewhat on the nature of their creed, at least on 'Gooroo Govind's' exposition of it. Hardy in frame, fierce in nature when aroused and when the welfare of the 'Khâlsa'[1] was at stake, it would be difficult to find an Oriental nationality producing better soldiers than the 'Sikhs.' We have proved them, as foes, full worthy of our steel, and as friends, let the ramparts of Delhi and Lucknow, the plains of China, and many a rugged hillside on the Affghan frontier, tell of their worth and valour. In instituting a comparison with the troops of Western nations, one would couple the 'Sikhs' with the British for enduring valour and steadiness, while the 'Puthân' might

[1] An Arabic term, literally Pure, Free, used to denote the 'Sikh' body politic.

be likened to the French for 'élan,' but, as I think, like the French also, without the dogged pluck which does not know when it is beaten. If we do come to loggerheads with the 'Russ,' we may reckon on the 'Sikhs,' under British leading, for holding their own side by side with our troops.

The 'Sikhs' are excellent agriculturists, though in this respect they are hardly equal to some of the less warlike races.

The 'Sikh' religion holds somewhat of the same relation to the Hindoo faith as the Wahâbee schism does to the creed of Mohammed. According to Gooroo Govind's exposition, all old forms were useless. God was one and indivisible. Idolatry was abomination, and Mohammedanism to be destroyed. The 'Wahâbees,'[1] except of course in the last particular, hold much the same views. They will allow none of the doctrines which associate 'Mohammed' with the Deity, holding him to have been a mere mortal. They abjure anything like idolatry in the paying of honours to deceased saints, or erecting mausoleums over their remains, and admit of no repetitions of prayers over rosaries or beads. As a matter of religious practice, the smoking of tobacco is unlawful, which finds its parallel in the 'Sikh' belief, a true 'Sikh' never touching it. It should be mentioned, however, that the prohibition in the 'Sikh' religious writings is confined to snufftaking, but the practice of abstention from smoking also has been general.

The tenets of the 'Sikh' faith are developed in the

[1] Abdul Wahâb, the first prophet of the sect, flourished in about 1760.

'Adee Gurunth,' or first book of Nânuk, the first religious teacher, and those of his successors to the ninth Gooroo, Tegh Buhâdur, and in the 'Duswén Pâdshah ki Gurunth,' or book of the tenth ruler, Gooroo Govind. There are also other writings of 'Nnuk' and 'Govind' which have religious authority. The general tenor of the doctrine inculcated is belief in the one God, and the observance of purity, truth, and charity. The ceremonial forms of the Brahmins are prohibited and contemned, and the slaying of Mohammedans, or, as they are called in the religious writings, 'Toorks,' is considered a good deed, as recorded above.

Here perhaps should be noticed a branch of 'Sikh' schismatics known as 'Kookas,' who caused a good deal of trouble in 1871. This sect came into existence about a quarter of a century ago. Like most reformers, Oriental and other, they professed a stricter discipline and a higher aim than the parent creed. One 'Ram Singh' was the head of the community in 1871, the sect having originated in 1847, shortly before the annexation of the Punjaub. They were as a rule quiet and orderly, and the sect attracted little notice until about 1862-63, when their increasing numbers, and rumours of political agitation designed by the party, called the attention of the Government to their proceedings. The apostle 'Ram Singh' was arrested, or rather kept under surveillance, but at the end of three or four years, no tangible proofs of conspiracy having been discovered against him, he was released, and the Punjaub Government, with the natural desire of viewing all things in the brightest colours, reported in

1866-67 that 'the conduct of "Ram Singh" and his followers, since his release, had been excellent' (Report 1866-67, par. 328). But this 'excellence' did not long continue. In June and July 1871, two organised assaults were made by members of the 'Kooka' sect on the Mohammedan butchers of 'Umritsur' and 'Loodiânah' respectively. Four Mohammedans were murdered in the first, and several killed and dangerously wounded in the second onslaught. The sentence of death passed on those of the perpetrators who were discovered and convicted would, it was hoped, have a salutary and deterrent effect upon the sect, but this expectation was not fulfilled.

In January 1872, a numerous body of 'Kookas' attacked 'Maloudh,' a small town in the 'Loodiânah' district, with a view of getting arms to enable them to assault the town of 'Maler Kotla,' belonging to a Mohammedan chief. After doing some damage at 'Maloudh' they were repulsed, and moved on to attack 'Maler Kotla.' After a sharp conflict, in which several of the defenders of the place were killed, the 'Kookas' were beaten back and took refuge in the jungle, where they were subsequently apprehended. The Deputy Commissioner (Mr. Cowan) arrived shortly after, and after consultation with the native chiefs who were present, 'Maler Kotla' being in independent territory, he determined to make a severe example of the 'Kookas' engaged in this unprovoked assault, in the hope of striking dread into the rest of the body, who were, it was said, meditating a general movement. Mr. Cowan therefore ordered all the 'Kookas' concerned in the 'Maler Kotla' affair to be blown away from guns, which was duly carried into effect, leaving sixteen who had attacked 'Maloudh,' which was in British territory, to be tried by the Commissioner, Mr. Forsyth. These were tried formally the following day, found guilty, and sentenced to the same punishment as the others. A great outcry was made at the time against what was called the barbarity of these sentences, and Mr. Cowan was dismissed from the service, and Mr. Forsyth removed from his appointment.

There can be no doubt, however, that the promptness and determination displayed by these officers saved the Government from a complication which, if they had allowed the law to run its tedious course, might have assumed a very serious form. The hard measure dealt out to these gentlemen was much commented on at the time, and men in office did not hesitate to say, that if this were the treatment to be expected for loyally doing duty to the Government, the Government might 'kill the next Percy itself.' It is probable that if Mr. (now Sir Douglas) Forsyth and Mr. Cowan had disposed of these rebels and murderers *morè Anglico* by hanging them, they would have been applauded on all sides, but because they resorted to the native mode of punishment, which was unfamiliar to English ideas, therefore they were deemed guilty of barbarity. One by no means desires to be an apologist for unnecessary savageness in punishment, but no one will deny that a prompt and severe example was necessary in this case, where the 'Kookas' were in open rebellion against the Government, and in the course of which they had murdered several unarmed and unoffending subjects of that Government. And further, it may be fairly assumed that if the culprits themselves had been consulted as to the mode of their execution, every one of them would have preferred the death at the cannon's mouth to being sent out of the world by the hands of the common hangman, who is religiously unclean. Be that as it may, there can be no doubt that the Government reaped the benefit of their officers' energetic action in the complete quelling of the 'Kookas,' who have never shown front since; and if Mr. Cowan's prospects have been ruined, and Sir Douglas Forsyth has been made a rolling stone of ever since, it is only the way of the world—

> 'The page slew the boar,
> The peer had the gloire.'

A brief notice of the causes which led to the Sikh invasion of British India in 1845, and which entailed the occupation, and subsequent annexation, of the Punjaub, may not be out of place here.

As has been noticed above, the death of 'Runjeet Singh' in 1839 was followed by anarchy and confusion in the 'Sikh' state. Among the aspirants to the throne there was no one of sufficient capacity to secure the succession for himself. Among the reputed sons of Runjeet Singh was Sher Singh, supposed to be the offspring of his wife 'Muhtâb Kour,' but there were strong doubts, said to have been shared by Runjeet himself, as to whether she had ever borne a son. The story at the time was, that Muhtâb Kour was really delivered of a daughter during 'Runjeet's' absence on a warlike expedition, and that on his return she presented to him as his own twin-sons, Sher Singh and Tára Singh, the offspring respectively of a carpenter and a weaver. Whether there was any truth in the rumour or not, 'Sher Singh' was brought up as the son of 'Runjeet,' and at the latter's death put in his claim to the succession. But there was an elder claimant in the person of 'Khuruk Singh,' born to Runjeet in 1802, and he was recognised as the successor by the British Government. His son, Nao Nihâl Singh, however, exercised the real authority during the brief period of Khuruk Singh's reign, about eighteen months.

In speaking of this portion of 'Sikh' history, it becomes necessary to notice briefly the 'Jumoo' Rajas, as they were called, who played a conspicuous part in this turbulent period, and one of whom, Goolâb Singh, was destined to be brought into close political connection with the British Government thereafter.

The Jumoo Rajas were brothers, three in number. Goolâb Singh, the eldest, a man of great craft and ambition, but cautious withal, who kept himself aloof from the purlieus of the court, content to advance the interests of the family by his intrigues at a distance.

The second brother, 'Dhiân Singh,' had not probably the talent of Goolâb Singh, but he had all his ambition, and devoted his energies to securing for himself the post of 'Wuzeer,' which he succeeded in obtaining, and with it a considerable influence over the mind of the Maharaja, Runjeet Singh.

'Sochait Singh,' the third brother, appears to have been rather a *bon camarade* and gallant soldier than a diplomatist, and displayed no special talents of any kind.

The origin of the brothers was obscure, though Goolâb Singh claimed noble descent. It is certain, however, that they commenced their career as soldiers and running footmen in Runjeet Singh's service in about 1820, and from that low degree raised themselves to the position of special favourites of the Maharaja.

'Runjeet Singh' conferred upon them the province of 'Jumoo' in fief, and they thence derived the title of the 'Jumoo' Rajas. At Runjeet Singh's death they espoused at first the cause of Khuruk and Nao Nihâl Singh, though the latter was secretly hostile to them, and dreaded their rapidly increasing power and influence. He was glad to make use of them, however, and effected through their means the assassination of Chait Singh, his father Khuruk Singh's favourite. Nao Nihâl Singh's subsequent machinations to get rid of the 'Jumoo' Rajas were not destined to be successful.

In less than a year and a half after Runjeet Singh's death, Khuruk Singh died, worn out and effete, though not an old man, and very shortly after, on his return from performing the funeral rites of his father, Nao Nihâl Singh was killed by the fall of a masonry gateway, under which he was passing on an elephant. It was surmised by some that this was a shrewd contrivance of the 'Jumoo' brothers to get rid of one whose power was daily increasing, and whose hostility to their family had been clearly manifested.

On Nao Nihâl Singh's death, Sher Singh renewed his pretensions to the throne, with the support of the Jumoo Rajas, and after a brief interval, during which the claims of Dhuleep Singh, whose existence was not known to the British Government before the end of 1840, were advanced, Sher Singh succeeded to the throne about the end of January 1841, Dhiân Singh occupying the post of Wuzeer.

Sher Singh's tenure of power was almost as brief as that of his predecessor, Khuruk Singh.

He was murdered by Ajeet Singh on 15th September 1843. His son, Purtâb Singh, was slain at the same time by Ajeet's uncle, and the massacre was completed by the assassination of Dhiân Singh, the Wuzeer. The death of the latter was amply avenged by his son, Heera Singh, who assumed the office of Wuzeer, and caused Dhuleep Singh to be proclaimed Maharaja.

Thus, in the brief space of four years, the 'Sikh' state had witnessed the removal by assassination of three of its supreme rulers, and to these may be added Dewan 'Sâwun Mull,' the able governor of the province of Mooltan, in which post he was succeeded by his son, Moolrâj, who played a prominent part in the war of 1848-49.

But it is time to speak of a body whose influence had been gradually increasing since the death of Runjeet Singh, and which had now become the paramount power in the Sikh state.

As in the decline of the Roman Empire, the army, represented by its lawless and ambitious leaders, had directed and controlled the affairs of the state, so at the period of the approaching extinction of the 'Sikh' power, the military body became supreme in authority, directing the councils of the nation.

During Runjeet Singh's lifetime, the army had been

THE 'SIKH' ARMY.

his willing and obedient instrument for extending the dominions and enhancing the influence of the 'Khâlsa,' but after his death, when, as has been stated, there was no individual of sufficient power of will to control and regulate their action, the army assumed a leading position in the state, and established an organisation for its own self-government, and for its transactions in reference to the civil administration.

This organisation was termed the 'Punchayut,' or council of five, and consisted of an elective body chosen from each battalion, through whom all the dealings of the military with the civil power were transacted; and from the time of which we now treat till the final overthrow at Sobrâon, this body exercised the paramount influence in the state.

After the death of 'Dhiân Singh,' his son, 'Heera Singh,' occupied the post of Wuzeer until 1844, when he also was slain, having become obnoxious to the soldiery. He was succeeded in the office of Wuzeer by 'Jowahir Singh,' the maternal uncle of the young Raja, 'Dhuleep Singh,'—'Lal Singh,' the reputed paramour of the Rânee Jundân Kour, being associated with him in the office. Neither of these men were endowed with energy or talent sufficient to deal with the difficulties of the time, and 'Jowahir Singh' becoming unpopular with the army, mainly through the intrigues of his coadjutor, 'Lal Singh,' was put to death by sentence of the 'Punchayut.' . 'Lâl Singh' was then nominated Wuzeer, and Raja 'Tej Singh' commander in chief.

The course of events has now brought us to November 1845. It had been evident to the British Government for some time past that the predominance of the army in the 'Sikh' state, with no responsible or efficient head to control its movements, would entail ere long a collision between the two Powers, and measures were taken to strengthen the garrisons of North-West India with troops and munitions of war. These were held by the Sikhs to be aggressive movements rather than simple measures of defence, and served to excite the restless spirit of the soldiery, whose sentiments of dislike and suspicion had already been aroused against the British Government in consequence of the latter having escheated a large sum of money which had been deposited by Raja 'Sochait Singh' in Ferozepore, and which was discovered after his death.

It was not difficult to stir up a restless and lawless body like the 'Sikh' soldiery to enter on hostilities against the British, especially if, as was generally supposed, the political leaders urged them on in the hope of the entire discomfiture of the army by the British, and of their being able to secure profitable terms for themselves from the victors. The rats had discovered that the house was tottering to its fall.

The 'Sikh' army crossed the Sutlej river on 11th December 1845, numbering from 30,000 to 40,000 men, and with 100 to 150 guns. To meet this attack the British commander had about 16,000 men and 60 or 70 guns.

Then followed the doubtful victories at Moodkee and Ferozshuhur. In the latter action defeat seemed almost certain, if, as has been before noticed, Raja 'Tej

Singh' had led on his reserves on the morning of 22nd December.

On the 21st January 1846, the British force under Sir Harry Smith encountered and repulsed a large body of the Sikhs at Buddowal, sustaining, however, the loss of all their baggage. This mishap was retrieved by the victory at Aliwal on 28th January; and the final success at 'Sobraon,' on 10th February, dispersed for the time the 'Sikh' army, and left the road to Lahore open to the conquerors.

CHAPTER III.

Administration of the Punjaub under a British Resident—Intrigues against the British by the Rânee—Siege of Mooltan—Battles of Ramnuggur and Chiliânwâla—Final victory at Goojerât and annexation of the Punjaub.

THEN came the difficulty of managing a country whose body politic comprised so many discordant elements. The army, which had been supreme, had for the time received its 'quietus,' but still contained the elements of grave disquiet, destined to give trouble at a future period.

The immediate results of the British victories were the cession by the 'Sikhs' of the Jullundar Dooâb (the delta between the Sutlej and Béâs rivers), and the hill countries between the Béâs and Indus, including Cashmere, to the British Government. The first-named tract was immediately occupied by us, and brought under direct British administration. The greater portion of the latter country, including Cashmere, was made over to Raja 'Goolâb Singh' of 'Jumoo' in perpetuity, in consideration of a sum of one million to be paid to the British by him. In addition to the above, a treaty was effected between the two states, by which the administration of the Sikh government during 'Dhuleep Singh's' minority was to be carried on by a Council of Regency, assisted by a British Resident, which latter should 'have full authority to direct and control all matters in every department of the state.'

With these plenary powers, the British Resident, assisted by a large establishment of subordinate officers, commenced his work.

Of the Resident, it need only be recorded that his name was Henry Lawrence.

Of the subordinates, many became well known to fame afterwards.

Herbert Edwards, whose military talents helped us so effectually in the subsequent outbreak of 1848-49, whose administrative power on the Peshawur frontier for several years, and whose unyielding pluck and felicitous management in the Mutiny of 1857, exercised so large an influence in the saving of the country. Nicholson, the strong of will and firm of purpose, whose name was a battle-cry. Arthur Cocks, the energetic civilian but born soldier, who played a soldier's part at Goojerât, where he was severely wounded. The chivalrous Reynell Taylor, Vans Agnew, whose noble death confirmed the high promise of his life;—these and many more were the chosen supports of the noble chief to whose hands was intrusted the difficult and delicate task of renovating a well-nigh ruined country.

The work opened favourably. Regular courts of justice, a thing unknown heretofore in 'Sikh' annals, were established. Officers were set to work immediately to assess the land revenue on fair and equitable terms. The military system was placed on a more regular footing, and all practicable measures were adopted for ensuring the advantages of regular government. But the unsettled passions of the 'Sikhs' were not to be quieted down by one series of reverses, heavy and almost overwhelming though they had been. The spirit of intrigue was at work, instigated chiefly, perhaps, by the Maharaja's mother, 'Jundân Kour.'

Deprived of her paramour, 'Lâl Singh,' whose banishment was one of the points insisted on in the treaty of 1846, checked in her extravagant and licentious career by the presence of the British element in the administration, and reduced to insignificance as far as her political influence was concerned, the Rânee set to work to undermine the influence of the British, and to stimulate the turbulent spirit of the 'Khâlsa' to fresh attempts against the dominant power. No long period elapsed before the machinations of the 'Rânee' and the other conspirators bore fruit. The first blow was the murder of Vans Agnew and Anderson at Mooltan, assistants to the Resident, who had been sent to inquire into the conduct of 'Moolrâj,' the Dewân or superintendent of that province, who was suspected of fraudulent dealing in his administration, and who had been summoned to Lahore to render an account of his management.

These transactions commenced in April 1848, about two years after the location of the Resident at Lahore.

The first measures taken by our Government were to deport the Rânee from Lahore, and thus remove a most mischievous influence from our midst. She was taken across the Sutlej at the end of May 1848, and sent down under a strong escort first to Benares, from whence she was removed to the fort of Chunâr.

The next step was to move a force upon Mooltan, where Moolrâj, supported by a considerable body of soldiers of the Khâlsa and miscellaneous levies, had determined to hold out the strong fort of Mooltan against the expected attack.

The siege proved a more difficult task than had been anticipated, and it was soon found that the force which had been just sent under General Whish was not sufficient either in numbers or material to effect the capture of the place. Reinforcements both in men and guns became necessary, and the siege was protracted from August to December.

Meanwhile a large force under 'Chutur Singh Atâreewâla' had raised the standard of revolt in Huzarah and the north-western provinces of the Punjaub, and this leader was soon joined by his son, 'Sher Singh,' from Mooltan, with a powerful reinforcement, and the united body commenced to move towards Lahore at the end of November 1848.

Meanwhile the British had been assembling their forces at Lahore to meet these complications, and about the second week in December the army under the command of Sir Hugh Gough moved across the Râvee to encounter the 'Sikh' rebel force. The 'Sikhs' had by this time crossed the 'Jhelum,' and were in force on the right bank of the Chenaub, their main camp resting at 'Moong,' near the Jhelum.

The campaign opened disastrously for the British. The enemy were first encountered at Ramnuggur, a village on the left bank of the 'Chenaub' river, in front of which the 'Sikhs' had thrown out a considerable body of skirmishers, covered by their guns on the opposite bank, and protected in great measure by ravines running down to the river from the direction of Ramnuggur. Our cavalry were thrown forward with the intention of driving these skirmishers across the river (then fordable), but became entangled in the ravines, and suffered severely from the fire of the 'Sikh' marksmen, who were concealed among the cover afforded by the irregularity of the ground. A very questionable victory was dearly purchased at the expense of the lives of Cureton and Havelock, the former perhaps the first cavalry officer of the day.

A portion of our force crossed the 'Chenaub' above 'Ramnuggur' shortly after, and after the desultory action of 'Sadoolapoor,' was joined by the main body, and the united force moved forwards in the direction of the Sikh camp. On the 13th January 1849, the British force was moving to take up its ground, when its progress was arrested by the fire of the Sikh heavy guns. Prophets after the fact urged that the force should have taken up ground for the night out of range, and the battle have been postponed till the morrow. It was now 3 P.M., only about two hours of daylight remained, and the position was most unfavourable for an attack from the broken character of the ground, which was undulating, and much obstructed in parts by thick jungle. Besides, the enemy had the

BATTLE OF 'CHILIÁNWÁLA.' 31

advantage of knowing our position, while his own formation was concealed from us by the jungle.

It was resolved, however, to make the attack, and the troops were deployed for the purpose at once. Difficult as it must always be to write the history of a battle, to record the order of events in this action of 'Chiliânwâla' is simply impossible. The position of the enemy at the commencement of the action was, as above noted, unknown, so it was impossible to make any advantageous disposition of our own forces to out-manœuvre them. All that remained to do, since fighting was determined on, was to send the British troops ahead until they felt the clash of their enemy's steel, a manœuvre not unfrequently adopted by Lord Gough in his Indian battles. The foe was soon found, and then commenced a game of hammer-and-tongs, our troops losing all the advantage which superior discipline and organisation might have secured to them, in consequence of their fighting in the dark as to their enemy's position and numbers, and in the midst of a jungle which foiled all attempts at regular formation. In the *pêle-mêle* which ensued there was some confusion in the cavalry movements, which need not be further noticed here. The infantry stood to it manfully. In numberless instances the enemy had so penetrated our line that the front and rear ranks had to 'form square' on one another to repel the attacks which were made on all sides; and when darkness put an end to the confusion, all we could boast of was that the British army stood on the same ground it had occupied when the fight began. Our loss was frightful. The 24th suffered more than any other regiment. When the cessation of the strife allowed the melancholy task of collecting the dead to be undertaken, the bodies of thirteen officers of this regiment lay in stark repose on the mess-table. Other regiments suffered nearly as severely, and no result had been obtained for all this butchery. The enemy retired in comparatively good order to his position on the Jhelum, and we were unable to follow up the advantage, if we can so term it, which we had gained. It was several days before confidence was restored, and we remained halted without moving to attack the 'Sikh' force, which lay encamped not very far from us. In fact, it was considered desirable to wait for the reinforcement which was expected shortly from Mooltan, that fort having at last been taken, which liberated some 6000 men to join the main force at Chiliânwâla.

The 'Sikhs,' taking heart at our inaction, commenced a flank movement with the intention of marching on Lahore, which was almost destitute of troops, and this move, if successful, might have resulted in the gravest consequences. It would have raised up in an instant all the scattered fragments of the 'Khalsa' in the 'Manjah,' or country about Lahore and Umritsur, and have exposed these two principal cities to sack and waste; and as we had nothing fit to be called a reserve available—the last European regiment at Lahore, the 53rd, having been moved up to join the army—it would have struck a blow at our prestige which might have been irreparable.

Fortunately the succours from Mooltan arrived in time to prevent these calamities. The force at 'Chili-

BATTLE OF 'GOOJERÂT.'

ânwâla' fell back on the 'Chenaub,' and effected its junction with the Mooltan division. This change of position brought the river 'Chenaub' on the right flank of the British army, and its front to the Sikhs, whose intention was to cross the river to the east of the town of 'Goojerât,' and move direct on Lahore.

Finding this movement checked by the new position taken up by the British, the 'Sikhs' prepared to give battle, and on the 26th of February 1849 the battle of Goojerât followed. This was fought on a different plan to that which had been pursued by Lord Gough in previous actions. Instead of, as at Maharajpoor, Ferozshuhur, and Chiliânwâla, the troops being sent straight at the guns of the enemy in position, without an effectual use of the arm of artillery in which we were so strong, the battle of Goojerât had some claim to be entitled an artillery action. As usual, we had to deliver the attack on the enemy in position; but, under Sir John Cheape's direction, such good use was made of the grand force of artillery with the army, that the 'Sikh' batteries were soon silenced, and our cavalry and infantry made their advance on fair terms with the foe. The sabre and bayonet soon disposed of the enemy's opposition, and before nightfall the Sikh force was utterly routed. Numbers dispersed after the action, and the only body which retained any semblance of cohesion was a force of 15,000 or 16,000 men under the principal leaders, which made off in the direction of Peshawur. A body of Affghan cavalry, which had joined the 'Sikhs' before 'Goojerât,' fled incontinently from the field, and hardly drew bridle till they reached the shelter of the 'Khyber' Pass. A flying division under Sir Walter Gilbert was immediately sent in pursuit of the Sikh fugitives, and overtook them between the Jhelum and Peshawur. They surrendered at discretion, and thus the *coup de grâce* was given to the supremacy of the Sikh 'Khalsa.'

On the 31st March following, the annexation of the Punjaub was publicly proclaimed, and one more province added to the British Empire.

It seems hardly worth while, at this distance of time, to reconsider the arguments for and against the annexation of the Punjaub. The question was much discussed at the time, and its advisability of course questioned by the peace-at-any-price party. It may be sufficient to say that the measure was wholly unpremeditated, and was forced on us by circumstances; and further, it is highly probable that, if we had not annexed the 'Sikhs,' they would have done their best to annex us!

They were the aggressors in the first instance; and unless the final measure of absorbing the 'Sikh' state into the British Empire had been promptly and thoroughly carried out, we should have had a continual recurrence of aggressions to meet and invasions to repel, which, judging from the experience of Ferozshuhur and Chiliânwâla, might have cost us dearly in the end, independently of keeping up a constant state of alarm and excitement in our Indian provinces.

It is not within the present purpose to write of the internal administration of the Punjaub since the annexation of the country, but rather of its external political relations. Let it suffice to say, that the efforts of many succeeding able administrators have been successful, not only in rescuing the province from ruin, but in bringing it into a state of almost unprecedented prosperity. The land revenue has been equitably assessed, rights of property defined, trade developed, the more heinous character of crime reduced to a minimum, the people as a rule are prosperous and contented; and some years ago few people would have been inclined to question the right of the Punjaub to be called the model province. But it has suffered, like all the rest of India, from over-legislation and over-government, and being younger than the sister provinces of Agra, Bengal, &c., it is likely to feel the infliction more. The present rage for statistics and percentages is likely to choke better work, and instead of a district officer being, as he used to be, a popular administrator in the best sense of the word, he is likely to degenerate into a beast of burden.

The present idea appears to be to make administrators machines as far as practicable, to discourage all individual effort, and to reduce the agents of Government to the condition of puppets, the chief at the central office pulling the wires. We pass on to consider the relations of the Punjaub on the north-west frontier.

CHAPTER IV.

Geographical description of north-west frontier—The Affghans—Their political relations—The 'Jirgahs'—Comparison of the Affghans with the Americans of Cortes's time—Affghan independence of Câbul—Description of the Pathân tribes — The 'Chigurzye'—'Hussunzye'—The Mudah Khail and Amayze—The 'Judoons'—Bonairs—Swâtees—Momunds—Bâjousees.

THE northern and western boundaries of the Punjaub are formed, as before described, by the mountain ranges of the 'Himalayas,' from 'Simla' on the north-east, to the 'Suleimani' range and its spurs on the 'Scinde' frontier to the westward.

It is difficult to give an exact estimate of the distance from point to point, as the line of boundary is extremely irregular, but 800 miles may be roughly assumed as the extent of frontier. Of this, an extent of about 280 miles is inhabited by Hindoo, and the remaining 520 by Mohammedan races. It is with the latter that we are now concerned; and the point of division of the two sects may be generally assumed as a line drawn from 'Murree' in British territory to 'Sirinaggar' in Cashmere, or still more widely, the river Indus, the countries to the west being Mohammedan, those to the east of the river Hindoo or Buddhist. Neither of these divisions are exact as regards the Mohammedans, many being found in tracts on the east of the Indus; but as regards the Hindoos, the river may be accepted as a well-defined boundary.

Our 'Hindoo' or 'Buddhist' neighbours give us as a rule no trouble whatever, either diplomatically or in a military point of view. The tribes which inhabit the lofty ranges to the north-east are thinly populated and of peaceful habits, and the kingdom of Cashmere, which intervenes between them and the Mohammedans, is a friendly if not a subject state. It is as our border approaches the Indus that we are brought into contact with troublesome and frequently hostile neighbours; and the following remarks will include, for general purposes, the whole of the 'Affghan' or 'Pathân' tribes,[1] from our frontier district of 'Huzârah' to the point of junction of the 'Pathân' and 'Bilooch' races at the southern extremity of the 'Derah Ismail Khan' district. It is not proposed to enter upon a history of the Affghan race here; that has been already effected by more qualified writers, and to those interested in that subject I would cite Burnes's 'Affghanistan' and Major James's 'History of the Peshawur Settlement,' as affording full and interesting details. The object in the present sketch is to show how the Affghans conduct themselves towards us as neighbours, and to illustrate our dealings with them in the like capacity.

To arrive at a fair estimate of the character of the

---

[1] These terms may be used almost indifferently—the first signifying an inhabitant of Affghanistan; the second, one speaking the Pushtoo language.

Affghans' conduct and dispositions towards us, we must first consider their condition politically and socially among themselves. We use the comprehensive appellation 'Affghans' in common parlance, as we should say Englishmen, Frenchmen, Germans, or Russians; but the plural term to denote a nation has a very different signification, when applied to the first, to what it holds when used with reference to European bodies. In the latter case, we understand the representative of a united body, under one form of government, and actuated by common interests. But the Affghans are split up into numberless political bodies, with, as a rule, no common interests, and acknowledging no common ruler. The only universal tie, in fact, is the religious one, all being members of the same creed, but this affects in only a secondary degree their political relations. Of course, if the faith of Islâm were threatened, and a 'jehâd' or general religious crusade proclaimed, there would be a certain amount of unity of action among them, but even then the fact of their being so unaccustomed to regular government, and the jealousies that would be excited against any one member of the body who might attempt to take a decided lead among them, would render the term of cohesion probably a brief one. Many tribes have their chief so called, but the obedience rendered to him is nought, and if his measures should run counter to the wishes of the majority of the tribe, they would speedily be set aside. There is one exception to this rule in the 'Akhoond' of 'Swât,' whose influence over the tribes of 'Bonair' and 'Swât,' which border the 'Yusufzye' section of the Peshawur district is very marked, as he unites the priestly and chieftain functions in one; and, for purposes of defence, we have found to our cost, as in the Umbelah campaign, that his power of collecting and keeping together a large number of both the tribes, and assembling others to meet a hostile demonstration, is very great; but it may be doubted if even his influence, which is in a great measure personal, would suffice to ensure continued united action, especially in offensive movements, of the tribes which he governs.

But although there is no individual government among the tribes, each has its 'jirgah,' or council of elders, who are supposed to represent the views and interests of the community. The 'jirgah' is composed of the greybeards and men of chief influence among the tribes. There is, it is believed, no regular elective process in the constitution of the 'jirgah,' nor is the office necessarily hereditary, though a son would probably succeed his father in the 'jirgah,' supposing him to possess the same qualifications. It is through the 'jirgah' that all political transactions are carried on with the tribe by the British officers, even though there should be a nominal chief in the background; and even at the close of the Umbelah campaign, when the 'Akhoond' was present in person, the peace negotiations were carried on through the 'Swat' and 'Bonair' 'jirgahs,' without direct reference to him, though he doubtless influenced their counsels to a considerable extent.

The tribe generally, but not invariably, accepts the decision of the 'jirgah,' and it is a matter of policy therefore, to work upon their fears or interests, and perhaps, above all, on their jealousies; for the 'Pathâns,' tricky and insincere themselves, regard even their own tribesmen with suspicion.

An amusing story, showing how these feelings can be worked on with advantage, is told of Major James, the Commissioner of Peshawur, who brought the negotiations at 'Umbelah' to a successful issue. Shortly before the last British victory at 'Lâloo,' the tribes came in to negotiate for terms, represented by their respective 'jirgahs.' At the time appointed for the conference, they presented themselves at the Commissioner's quarters, and were admitted separately in succession. The first 'jirgah' came in, seated themselves in due form in front of the Commissioner, and waited patiently for him to open the proceedings. He continued calmly writing at the table, and said not a word. After about half an hour had elapsed, he signified to the 'jirgah' that they were dismissed, and they were escorted out of the tent by the attendants, with all due form and ceremony. A second and a third were ushered in, and dismissed in like manner. As each came out, they were immediately attacked by the representative bodies of the other tribes with the question, 'What did he say to you?' At the reply 'Nothing,' the suspicions of the others were immediately aroused that these had secured favourable terms for themselves, or perhaps a large present in money, to the detriment of their neighbours, and the effect was to instil suspicion and dissension among the different councils, to our advantage. The author does not vouch for the entire correctness of this story, but it is *ben trovâto*, and something like it actually did occur. It will serve to illustrate the kind of diplomacy our officers on the frontier have to deal with, and the weakness, not to say childishness, of the Affghan representative councils.

There is a passage in Robertson's 'History of America,' describing the political and social condition of the natives of that country at the time of 'Cortes,' which illustrates so well the condition of the Affghans at present, that it is worth transcribing *in extenso*.

'No visible form of government is established. The names of magistrate and subject are not in use. Every one seems to enjoy his natural independence almost entire. If a scheme of public utility is proposed, the members of the community are left at liberty to choose whether they will or will not assist in carrying it into execution. No statute imposes service as a duty; no compulsory laws oblige them to perform it. All their resolutions are voluntary, and flow from the impulse of their own minds. The first step towards establishing a public jurisdiction has not been taken in those rude societies. The right of revenge is left in private hands. If violence is committed, or blood shed, the community does not assume the power of either inflicting or of moderating the punishment. It belongs to the family and friends of the person injured or slain to avenge the wrong or accept the reparation offered by the aggressor. If the elders interpose, it is to advise, not to decide; and it is seldom their counsels are listened to, for as it is deemed pusillanimous to suffer an offender to escape with impunity, resentment is implacable and everlasting' (Robertson's 'America,' twelfth edition, p. 134).

This description, relating to the condition of a people three and a half centuries ago, fits exactly the manners of the Affghans at the present time. On the concluding portion of the quotation, regarding blood-feuds and the avenging of personal injuries, there will be more to say hereafter.

Generally, then, among the tribes which march with our frontier from Huzârah to the Bilooch border there is no suzerain or controlling power.

The Ameer of 'Câbul' pretends to some authority over certain tribes which intervene between British territory and the kingdom of Câbul, but he is cautious never to assert it in effect, and, as a fact, the tribes, with one or two exceptions, hold their own without care or concern for the views or wishes of the court of 'Câbul.'

It is obvious that, with communities like these, naturally hostile to us on account of our religion and apprehensive of our motives, ever dreading the approach of the 'Feringhee,' and the increased civilisation and more settled government which follow in his train,—with neighbours such as these, the management of our frontier presents difficulties which are not to be met by any fixed course of treatment based on political probabilities, or on our dealings with settled and civilised communities elsewhere. The circumstances are exceptional, the treatment must be exceptional also.

An endeavour will now be made to show briefly the

character and power of the tribes with whom we have to deal, taking them in geographical order from north to south. Our first 'Pathân' neighbours to the north are the inhabitants of a mountain tract on the east bank of the Indus known as the 'Black Mountain.' The principal tribes inhabiting this range and its spurs are the 'Chigurzye' and 'Hussunzye,' numbering, the former about 5000, the latter about 3000 matchlocks. The term 'matchlocks' is used to denote the number of fighting men, as we say sabres or bayonets in speaking of European troops, but it is by no means every Pathân warrior that can boast of a matchlock, many being obliged to rest content with knife and tulwar.[1] Neither of the tribes above mentioned bear a very high character for prowess, even among their co-religionists. Among the fastnesses and cliffs of their mountain home they are of course formidable to a certain extent, but in the open they are very little to be dreaded. As a sample of their valour, it may be mentioned that during the fighting at Umbelah in 1863, when the 'Swât' and 'Bonair' mountaineers were keeping up a constant attack on our position, in spite of daily and severe loss, the heroes of the Black Mountain, upon whom the 'Akhoond' of 'Swât' had laid religious pressure to assist in the ejection of the infidel, brought a large contingent to the help of the faithful, and the day after their arrival were sent by the 'Akhoond' to storm the 'Crag' piquet. This was the practice always adopted by the wily old priest, to send every fresh contingent into action at once, for the purpose probably of testing

[1] Sword.

their courage, and also to spare his own more immediate followers from 'Swât' and 'Bonair.' In consequence, the 'Chigurzye' and 'Hussunzye' made the usual promenade, but, unfortunately for them, their intended attack was known and prepared for, and they met with such a hot reception, that their anticipated triumph ended in a disastrous and disgraceful defeat, and these long-legged paladins of the Black Mountain vanished with great celerity from the scene of action, and were never again heard of in a body on the battlefield of 'Umbelah,' although the fighting continued for nearly two months after their discomfiture. In 1868 the 'Hussunzye' made a raid on our Huzârah frontier, and an expedition was organised against them, which turned out to be rather a *fiasco*, as we mustered some 4000 or 5000 men of all arms, but did not find an enemy to test their prowess, the 'Hussunzye' disappearing before our troops with the same celerity they exhibited at Umbelah, so that the military operations ended in a promenade like that of the King of France's men—they marched up the Black Mountain and down again. These circumstances are related to show how contemptible as a foe these northern Pathâns are.

Passing to the west bank of the Indus, we find the two Pathân tribes of 'Mudah Khail' and 'Amazye,' which border the country of our tributary chief of 'Tunâwul,' whose principal town is 'Umb' on the 'Indus.' The 'Mudah Khail' are to the north of 'Umb,' and the 'Amazye' inhabit the eastern slopes of the 'Mâhâbun' mountain trending towards the Indus. Neither of these tribes are of much political importance to us, the Mudah Khail being far distant from our frontier, and the 'Amazye' only mustering 1000 or 1200 matchlocks, besides being held in check by our 'Tunâwul' friends.

Following the west bank of the Indus to the 'Pihoor' ferry, and thence diverging to the westward, we come to the amphitheatre of hills which environ the Peshawur district, inhabited by a considerable number of tribes, more or less under the influence of the 'Akhoond' of 'Swât.' The nearest tribe to the 'Indus' are the 'Judoons' or 'Gudoons,' which is large in numerical strength, but by no means remarkable for prowess. They are a cunning, shifty lot, willing to intrigue at any one's bidding, if any advantage is likely to accrue to themselves, but not ready by any means to support their cause with the sword, and they are looked upon with indifference and contempt by other more warlike tribes.

After the 'Gudoons' come the 'Bonairs' or 'Bonair-wâl,' the 'Swâtees,' the 'Momunds,' and 'Bâjourees,' in geographical order, the territory of the Momunds extending to the 'Câbul' river, which forms the boundary between them and the 'Afreede' tribes. It should be noted here that only the chief comprehensive title of the respective tribes is given. Each is subdivided into numberless small sections of 'Zyes' and 'Khails,' the enumeration of which would only puzzle and embarrass the general reader.

It was from the tribes just mentioned that we experienced so strenuous an opposition in the Umbelah expedition of 1863, and it may be as well to sketch briefly the principal events connected with that campaign, as illustrating in some measure the character of the warlike operations we are obliged ever and anon to undertake against our troublesome neighbours on the north-west frontier, and showing at once our weakness and our strength in the manner of conducting these expeditions.

CHAPTER V.

Causes which led to the Umbelah campaign—The Hindostanee fanatics—Assemblage of the British force—Military and political difficulties—Occupation of Umbelah Pass by our troops—Constant state of warfare for two months—Final victory at 'Lâloo'—Lessons to be derived from this campaign—Notice of the 'Akhoond' of Swât.

THE military operations at Umbelah had their origin in the troublesome action of a body of expatriated Hindostanees, who had taken up their abode in a part of the 'Mâhâbun' mountain, which, as above noted, impinges on the Indus, where it washes our frontier district of '' Huzârah.' This body of Hindostanees was made up of refugees from 'Patna,' the hotbed of 'Wahâbeeism' in Bengal, and it had received accessions from the survivors of the Mutiny in 1857. The party numbered perhaps 600 or 700 fighting men, and they received countenance and protection from the tribes, partly from motives of hospitality, partly on religious grounds as being Mussulmans, and as being led by a 'Moolvie' of superior reputed sanctity, and in no small degree, perhaps, because of the known hostility of the Hindostanees to the British Government, which they lost no opportunity of displaying by carrying on intrigues with their countrymen at Patna, who regularly furnished funds for their support, and by stirring up disaffection among the Pathâns.

In the summer of 1863, this colony of Hindostanee fanatics made a move in advance by occupying a village on the banks of the Indus belonging to an offshoot of the 'Gudoon' tribes, and immediately adjoining our tributary of 'Umb,' thus threatening his country on the right, and British territory on the opposite bank of the Indus. Pressure was immediately brought to bear on the tribes to cause the ejection of the Hindostanees from their limits, but after much conference and interviewings of 'jirgahs,' it became evident that the tribes could not or would not comply with what, in this instance, was certainly the just demand of the British Government, that they should not afford asylum to those who were actively engaged in carrying on intrigues against its authority. As soon as it became certain that we could expect no assistance from the tribes in ejecting the Hindostanee refugees from their stronghold, but that rather the Pathân community was disposed to afford them countenance and refuge, it became necessary for us to take measures for the security of our frontier, independently of the views of the different tribes in the matter. Accordingly, a large force was assembled in October 1863, amounting to between 5000 and 6000 men, including—an unusual element in these border expeditions—two European regiments, the 71st Highlanders and the 101st Fusiliers, reinforced at a later date by the 7th Fusiliers and 93rd Highlanders. The plan of attack was much discussed

THE 'UMBELAH' EXPEDITION.

in both its military and political bearings, much difficulty attending both. The plan favoured by the political officers was to advance upon the Hindostanee stronghold by the east and south approaches of the 'Mâhâbun' mountain. The tribes in that direction were not so formidable as those likely to be encountered in the advance by 'Umbelah,' and it might have been hoped that, by avoiding any near approach to the 'Bonair' country, we should not have experienced any hostile demonstration from them or the 'Swâtees.' The physical difficulties of attacking the 'Mâhâbun' position were not probably greater than those which were subsequently encountered at 'Umbelah,' and we should have avoided, at any rate, the appearance of hostility, which our occupying the head of the 'Bonair' Pass gave to our excitable neighbours in that quarter.

It was argued on the other side, that the proper course was to occupy temporarily the country to the north of the 'Mâhâbun' mountain, so as to attack the Hindostanees from that side, and force them to fight with their backs to the plain, and operating on their line of retreat. In the former expedition against these fanatics under Sir Sydney Cotton in 1858, the assault had been made from the south and south-east, and it was urged the result had been to admit of their escaping into the hills after their defeat at 'Sitânah.' The latter plan, that favoured by the military authorities, was adopted, and on the 19th October 1863 our troops moved from the 'Yusufzye' plain to seize the 'Umbelah' or 'Soorkhâvee' Pass, and thence to occupy the 'Chumla' plain on the northern slope of the 'Mâhâbun' hill.

D

The strictest secrecy was observed as to the route our troops were to take, and a feint was made by the detachment of a brigade to the mouth of the 'Durrun' Pass, by which the British force entered the hills in 1858, as if that were to be the line of advance now. Further, the proclamations to the tribes detailing the objects for which we were about to enter the hills, and avowing the friendly intentions of the British Government towards themselves, were only issued on the 19th October, and the heads of our columns appeared at the summit of the 'Umbelah' Pass, and within hail of the Bonair limits, at daybreak on the 20th; so that if the proclamation had reached the tribe at all, they had clearly no time to consider their line of conduct, and, with true Pathân suspicion, they considered that we had literally and figuratively stolen a march upon them—which indeed was the case, the same supposed necessity of secrecy having been the cause of the withholding of the proclamations until it was too late for the tribes to consider them.

It is of course easy to be wise after the fact, but it admits of fair argument whether by an open and clear avowal of our intentions to the tribes before taking the initiative by entering their country, we might not have had a better chance of quieting their minds and minimising their opposition, than by the somewhat sharp practice we actually adopted. At any rate, the suspicions aroused by our precipitate movements called into action all the energies of the tribes threatened, and by the time the last body of troops had marched into camp on the crest of the Umbelah Pass on the 23rd October, the hostile combination of the tribes presented so formidable a front, that we were obliged to relinquish the plan of advancing into the 'Chumla' plain, and devote all our energies to maintain our hold of the precarious position we occupied. The sacrifice of all other interests to the requirements of secrecy and rapidity of movement now bore its unfortunate fruits. It was found that the reported openness of the 'Umbelah' Pass was a delusion, too much trust having been placed in the statements of native residents of the neighbourhood, who wittingly or unwittingly conveyed to our officers the impression that it was an easy defile, not only for the march of troops, but for the passage of the huge *impedimenta* which usually follow in the train of an Anglo-Indian army. What the character of the pass really proved to be let the following extract from General Chamberlain's despatch determine :—' As a road for troops it certainly presents great difficulties. The track lies up the bed of a stream encumbered with boulders and large masses of rock, and is overgrown with low trees and jungle.'

It had been intended that as soon as the whole force was assembled at the crest of the pass it should move forwards into the 'Chumla' plain, leaving a sufficient body to hold the pass, and a reconnaissance was made on 22nd October by a party of cavalry and infantry under the guidance of an engineer officer. The reconnoitring party was suffered to proceed some eight or ten miles into the valley without opposition, but on its return, the 'Bonairs,' who had gathered in considerable numbers on the heights above, came down in force, and made a determined attack upon the party. It was repulsed with some little loss, and the detachment regained the camp soon after nightfall. This demonstration in force by the 'Bonairs,' followed as it was shortly after by the gathering of all the neighbouring tribes in support of the 'Bonairs,' completely changed the character of the expedition, and it became necessary to exert all our strength to hold our own in the position we had occupied at the head of the Umbelah Pass, and trust to time and the effect of repeated repulses to wear out the resources of the motley host which had collected against us. From the 20th October to the 15th December our force held this position on the defensive, exposed every day to the matchlock fire of the scattered swarms around them, and occasionally to a determined and united attack on the more exposed picquets, which on one or two occasions fell into the enemy's hands for a brief period, but were always gallantly retaken, though at some loss. These grand attacks generally took place on a Friday, the Mohammedan holy day of the week.

To borrow a description from the 'Lady of the Lake'—

> 'Wild as the scream of the curlew,
> From crag to crag the signal flew;
> Instant through copse and heath arose
> Bonnets and spears and bended bows;
> On right, on left, above, below,
> Sprung up at once the lurking foe;
> From shingles grey their lances start,
> The bracken bush sends forth the dart;
> The rushes and the willow wand
> Are bristling into axe and brand;

> And every tuft of broom gives life
> To plaided warrior armed for strife.
> The signal garrisoned the glen
> At once with full five thousand men,
> As if the yawning hill to heaven
> A subterranean host had given.
> Watching their leader's beck and will,
> All silent there they stood and still,
> Like the loose crags whose threat'ning mass
> Lay tottering o'er the hollow pass.'

The coalition of tribes against us consisted of the 'Bonairs,' 'Swâtees,' 'Momunds' and 'Bâjourees,' who at a later period were joined by a large contingent from 'Dhér.' Besides these, the Black Mountain tribes, and others on the Indus, lent their countenance and occasional support to the opposition. It is difficult to give anything like an exact estimate of the numbers opposed to us at any one time, as they were constantly changing, some remaining to fight, others going home to fetch supplies. The General, after the final conflict at 'Laloo,' estimated the numbers opposed to our troops on 15th and 16th December at 15,000 men, but before this it is probable that numbers had left the confederacy, hopeless of effecting the discomfiture of the infidel; and Major James notes this point in his report, adding that 'among those who remained a mutual mistrust prevailed.' It may fairly be assumed, then, that our troops had to sustain for two months the determined and often desperate onslaughts of 20,000 men, who could select their own opportunity for attack, and who were themselves secure from molestation until brought into contact with us by their own act. The whole history of the campaign reads like a romance. The locality, a rough spur of the Himalayas, overhung by pine trees, craggy and wild like the incantation scene in 'Der Freischutz,' the 'Pathân' warriors, clad for the most part in long sombre blue garments, hovering like the demons in the play round the magic circle of our piquets, but not able to break in, while the constant rattle of the matchlock and rifle, and the occasional booming of the big guns, might well stand for the flashing of the lightning and the roar of the elements around the devoted Caspar. There was no romance, however, in the deeds of valour which were wrought in that hotly-contested mountain pass, and especially in and around the 'Crag' piquet. Though distributing their favours freely among the other defence posts of our camp, the 'Crag' piquet received a special share of the enemy's attention; it was thrice wrested for a brief space from our grasp, and it was in the recovering of this that special acts of dash and valour were exhibited by our troops.

Two Victoria crosses were won in the assault and recapture of this post by Pitcher, 1st Punjaub Infantry, and Fosbery, doing duty with the 101st Fusiliers. Two other officers, Keyes of the 1st, and Brownlow of the 20th Punjaub Infantry, were recommended by the General in command for this much-prized decoration, and why they did not get it is known best to the superior authorities. It was a glorious defence altogether, and though perhaps the deeds at the 'Crag' piquet, the 'Castle Dangerous' of the position, were the most notable, there were not wanting numberless instances of pluck, dash, and endurance at the other points, which would have reflected honour on any battlefield where Englishmen have won fame and honour.

We have been led perhaps into too long a discussion of this particular expedition, but it may be useful as showing what our troops in India can do under all disadvantages. Harassed by the constant attacks of an enemy whose vigilance never ceased, and to whose successive flow of reinforcements there seemed no limit, receiving the onset instead of delivering it, 'under arms, and on duty almost day and night,' and, as regards the native troops, fighting many of them against their own relatives, and opposed to their spiritual pastor, the Akhûnd—under all these hindrances of constant exposure, fatigue, severe loss occasionally, rupture of family and religious associations, these noble troops held their own for two weary months, and when their time came, rushed to the front, and swept away all opposition like the wind, and 'stood triumphant on the fatal hill,' like the heroes of Albuera. The result achieved by this campaign was of great importance. The 'Bonairs,' who had suffered more severely, as their bravery was more conspicuous, than their allies, agreed themselves to burn the stronghold of the Hindostanees at 'Mulka,' and for this purpose some of their chiefs, with a small contingent, and accompanied by Colonel Reynell Taylor, the Commissioner, and the corps of Guides, about 300 bayonets, marched on the 19th after the victory at Lâloo. They reached 'Mulka' on the 21st. The 'Amazye' tribe, in whose country 'Mulka' is situated, had assembled in large numbers on the hills above, as if with the intention of attacking the party.

Matters looked very serious, as our troops were vastly outnumbered, and of course quite isolated from the main force; but by the influence of the Bonair 'jirgah,' and the firm and determined bearing of Taylor, the 'Amazye' withdrew their opposition, and 'Mulka' was completely destroyed. The object of the expedition having been obtained, the tribes utterly discomfited and reduced to sue for peace, the force returned to the plains, after having, as noted by Major James, the Commissioner, completely asserted the power of the British Government 'before the largest, bravest, and most formidable coalition we have ever been called on to meet in the Trans-Indus territories.'

The lessons to be gathered from the 'Umbelah' campaign appear to be as follows:—

First, the danger of divided counsels. It will be seen, from what has been said above, that the civil and political bodies, represented by the Lieutenant-Governor, Colonel Reynell Taylor, and others, were in favour of advancing by the east and south of the 'Mâhâbun' mountain, where, though the difficulties of the country were as great, probably, as those by the 'Umbelah' route, the chances of being brought into hostile collision with the more powerful tribes were infinitely less; while the military authorities insisted on the 'Umbelah' route, mainly on the grounds that the line of the Hindostanees' retreat would be cut off by attacking the north front of the 'Mâhâbun' mountain. But this argument was hardly sufficient to outweigh the very palpable danger of throwing the invading force into such immediate proximity to the 'Bonair' tribe, the most powerful of the whole coalition. Neither, probably, would the object have been attained of cutting off the Hindostanees' retreat by a successful onslaught on the northern side of the 'Mâhâbun,' for the north-east and part of the eastern slopes of the mountain were still open to their line of retreat, and they could have found refuge with the 'Mudah Khail,' or, as some of them subsequently did, with the 'Hussunzye.'

Prophesying after the fact, it would seem that the attack by the south and east could not have landed us in worse difficulties than were experienced in the northern route, and they might have been avoided altogether.

Another instance of the danger of divided counsels in important transactions like these is to be found in the fact that the Lieutenant-Governor of the Punjaub, supported by the Military Secretary of the Supreme Government, Lord Elgin, the Governor-General, being then in a dying state, urged the withdrawal of the force from the Umbelah Pass to the plains. The effect of this would have been to have raised the whole border against us, and it would 'necessarily have committed us to a protracted campaign.' This order of the Lieutenant-Governor was sent on the 20th November, the day on which the last attack was made on our position, in which the enemy suffered so severely as to leave our troops entirely unmolested until the 15th December, when we ourselves assumed the offensive.

Fortunately, James and Chamberlain were men too firm of purpose to withdraw from a position, however dangerous or difficult, while a prospect of success remained, and as an option was left to them in the matter, they determined on maintaining the position, a resolution amply justified by the subsequent success. At the same time, in thus acting in opposition to the wishes of the Punjaub and Supreme Governments, they incurred a most grave responsibility, which might have been spared them.

Once more, at the critical moment, when all the circumstances on the spot tended to show that the time had come for us to make the much-longed for attack, the result proving the correctness of the views of those on the spot, the General commanding the force received a telegram from the Commander-in-chief, prohibiting him, in consequence of instructions received from the Supreme Government, from 'attempting any operations until further orders.' This also was fortunately overruled by a direct representation of the political authorities, but the permission to attack only arrived just in time; for the assault on Lâloo on the morning of 15th December anticipated by one day only an intended onslaught of all the tribes, which had been determined on by the Akhûnd in consequence of his having received large reinforcements, among them, it was said, 6000 matchlocks from 'Dhér.' The above were not the only differences of opinion. Another lesson to be learned from this expedition is, in any transactions with the hill tribes, political or military, always be prepared for the *worst*. Let no calculations based on our ideas of what is probable or reasonable enter into our action or dealings with them, or into our forecast of their probable line of action. If this caution had been observed before entering on the Umbelah campaign, our force probably would have consisted of ten instead of five thousand men, and we might then have moved straight to the accomplishment of that object, which, under different conditions, it took us two months to attain.

Thirdly, Let our dealings with the tribes be plainly and unmistakably open. It is better to risk somewhat by a distinct enunciation of our views and motives in dealing with the Affghans than to attempt to out-manœuvre them.

Thus the delay in the issue of the proclamation to the 'Bonairs,' from the much-insisted on necessity of secrecy, may have had the appearance to them of a trick; for, as Major James has noted in his report, for documents of this nature to be appreciated, time must be given to call the representatives of the tribes, that the matter may be discussed in council. 'Supposing therefore,' he adds, 'that the proclamations reached their destination, is it likely that a brave race of ignorant men would pause to consider the purport of a paper they could not read when the arms of a supposed invader were glistening at their doors?'

It may be as well, before quitting this part of the subject, to give a rough idea of who the Akhûnd of 'Swât' is, who exercised so powerful an influence in these transactions. The Persian term Akhûn or Akhûnd signifies a tutor or preceptor, and is applied, I believe, generally in a religious sense; and thus the 'Akhûnd' is considered as the chief religious head and authority, holding towards the people of 'Bonair,' &c.,

much the same position, *magnis componere parva*, as the 'Sheikh ul Islâm' at Constantinople does towards the general body of the faithful. The present 'Akhûnd' is a very aged man, said to be above ninety, but this extreme longevity seems hardly compatible with his energy both mental and physical. He has holden his present position for many years, and, as above noticed, exercises a most powerful influence over the clans on the north of the Peshawur valley, but he has rarely interfered in mundane matters. Indeed, until the embroglio in 1863, the only worldly affair in which he exerted his influence over the tribes was to induce the 'Swâtees' to accept 'Syud Akhbar Shah,' the friend and counsellor of 'Ahmud Shah,' the founder of the Hindostanee colony, as their king.

During the general convulsion which followed the outbreak of the Mutiny in 1857, and which reached to even these distant parts, the 'Akhûnd' is said to have counselled the disciples who resorted to him for advice not to enter upon any hostile demonstration against us; and certain it is that during that time of our great trouble, 'Swât,' often the cause of much anxiety, was quiet.

Major James considered that the Akhûnd was only brought into the field in 1863 by jealousy lest 'Moulvee Abdoolah,' the leader of the Hindostanee fanatics, should supplant him in his religious supremacy over the 'Bonairwâl.' His conduct and character have been much discussed in the Indian newspapers lately, in connection with our relations with the Ameer of Cabul, and he has been reported on one or two occasions to be organising a 'jehâd' or religious crusade against us, but his past career is so much against such an hypothesis, that until there are better grounds than native correspondents' reports for the rumour, one should be inclined to place little faith in it. The 'Akhûnd'[1] is a great ascetic, and lives a life of simplicity and devotion, and his influence may be considered as almost entirely personal. It is not likely that his son, if he should succeed him in the priestly office, will ever possess the power or authority exercised by the present 'Akhûnd.' Little is known of the son's character, but he has always been spoken of as far inferior in capacity and reputation to his father.

[1] Since the above was written the death of the Akhûnd has been reported.

CHAPTER VI.

The 'Bonairs'—Their fighting strength—The 'Momunds'—Their hostility to us—The 'Afreedees'—The 'Kohât' Pass—The 'Khutuks'—The 'Wuzeerees'—The 'Câbul Khail'—The 'Oomurzye'—Expeditions against those tribes—The 'Muhsoods'—Description of their country—Attack on our frontier by a large body of the tribe.

THE Bonairs are said to muster from 12,000 to 15,000 fighting men, the 'Swâtees' probably as many; and taking them and the remaining tribes to the Câbul river, the 'Momunds' and 'Bajourees,' we should not be much astray, perhaps, in fixing the whole number at from 40,000 to 50,000 men.

The 'Momunds' have often given us trouble on the frontier, unfavourably distinguished in this respect from the Bonairs and 'Swâtees,' who, the Bonairs especially, had conducted themselves as good neighbours until 1863.

The 'Momunds'' hostility towards us commenced at a very early date. The first report of the Punjaub Government in 1849 speaks of them as having already 'gained a notoriety by desultory skirmishing with British troops.' In 1851–52, they 'carried on a guerilla warfare, cutting up stragglers and attacking our villages during dark nights;' and finally a force of 6000 of them came down on our frontier post of 'Shubkuddur.' They were met, however, by Sir Colin Campbell (Lord Clyde) with a small force, and repulsed with loss. Thus they continued annoying our frontier till 1860-61, when their chief, 'Nuwâb Khan,' came in and tendered his submission, after which there was an interval of quiet until the 'Umbelah' business in 1863, when the 'Momunds' lent their aid to the Bonairs at Umbelah, and threatened our border at 'Shubkuddur.'

Since then the 'Momunds' have been tolerably peaceful neighbours. Many of the tribe hold lands within our border, and this is a source both of good and evil to our administration. The 'Momunds' are more under the influence and authority of the ruler of Câbul than any other frontier tribe, and in any demonstration against us, he would probably receive systematic support from this clan.

To pass on now to the numerous tribes, or rather assemblage of tribes, known as 'Afreedees,' a term which will be familiar even to many English readers, from their having seen so many accounts in the newspapers of our dealings with them in the matter of the Kohât Pass. There are numberless subdivisions of the tribe, which need not be enumerated here, as it will be sufficient for the purpose of this notice to designate them under the general appellation. The country of the 'Afreedees' commences from the right bank of the 'Câbul' river, and extends for about fifty miles nearly due south, and marching with our border the whole distance; and if its course were unbroken, we should probably not have more trouble with the 'Afreedees' than we experience from the rest of our 'Pathân' neighbours. But, as will be seen from a reference to the map, there is a tongue of 'Afreedee' land interposed between our two principal frontier stations of Peshawur and Kohât, directly traversing the line of communication between them. This defile, known generally as the 'Kohât' Pass, is some fifteen miles in length and three or four in breadth. Bleak, and in some places precipitous, hills flank the gorge, and it is altogether a troublesome and difficult bit of country to deal with—an expensive incumbrance, but 'politically indispensable to the British Government, as connecting Peshawur with our other Trans-Indus possessions.'

It appears that the resolution to keep this pass open by subsidising the 'Afreedees,' rather than to hold it ourselves by the construction of fortified posts, was adopted at the annexation of the Punjaub, as the first engagement with the 'Afreedees' was contracted in April 1849. The terms were that R.5700 (£570) per annum, which was subsequently increased for a time to £1370, were to be paid by the British Government to the Afreedee headmen, in consideration of which the latter bound themselves to maintain forty-five matchlockmen to hold the pass, to keep the pass open, and generally to be responsible for the security of the property and persons of travellers. The contract was hardly completed before it was broken by the attack of a body of Afreedees on a working party of our sappers and miners in the pass. This was retaliated by the movement of a body of troops under Sir Charles Napier, and the attack and capture of the Afreedee villages in the pass; but the lesson was not complete, and from that time till the present, an interval of twenty-seven years, scarcely a year has passed without witnessing some acts of robbery and murder on the part of the Afreedees, and of reprisals on our side. Numerous military expeditions have been organised against the clan during the quarter of a century which has elapsed since we first came into contact with them, but it would seem that they are as untamed and irrepressible as ever. The Punjaub Government, in each annual report, congratulates itself that the Afreedees are settling down to the character of peaceful neighbours and firm friends of the Government, while the succeeding annual *resumé* probably has to report some act of hostility on the part of the supposed penitents, which entails the application of the usual remedies, closing of the pass and stopping the trade of the delinquents as an alterative in mild cases, and the despatch of a military expedition as a drastic dose in more flagrant instances.

To illustrate this, the following quotation is given from the Punjaub Report of 1869-70, which should be read in the light of the events of the last two years in connection with the Kohât Pass, and of the formidable military expedition now (November-December 1877) organised against the Pass Afreedees. The Secretary is contrasting the happy state of affairs at the time of writing with that which prevailed in former years, and remarks, 'In Kohât *every one* of the numerous and powerful surrounding tribes has paid compensation for past offences, and sought the friendship of the British Government, while the Afreedees, formerly described as 'notoriously faithless,' have become, not probably from any change in their nature, but owing to their growing trade in British territory, the most faithful observers of their engagements.' The italics are the Secretary's own.

The conduct of the Pass and other Afreedees illustrates well what has been said above regarding the difficulty of dealing with such irresponsible agents.

Many of the acts which have brought us into collision with the tribe have been perpetrated by members of the community against the wishes of the main body, and yet, when the mischief is done, the whole clan are obliged to take the responsibility of it, as the idea of giving up a clansman to suffer punishment is almost unheard of; but I reserve further remarks on this head until we come to consider the whole question of frontier management. The number of fighting men among the 'Afreedees,' including the large tribe of 'Orukzye,' may amount probably to between 30,000 and 40,000.

The next tribe in geographical order are the 'Khutuks,' numbering, according to the estimate furnished by the Report of 1849-52, 15,000 fighting men. This is probably considerably above the mark. The tribe is not mentioned in the enumeration of frontier clans given in the Report for 1869-70; they are 'lumped' probably among the other 'Pathâns.' The conduct of this tribe presents a most singular contrast to that of their northern neighbours the 'Afreedees,' as well as to that of the 'Wuzeerees' on the south. These latter clans have kept us in continual hot water ever since the annexation of the country, whereas there is not a single instance, so far as the author is aware, of the Khutuks, *as a tribe,* having shown hostility to us; their quiescence has not proceeded from their being of a less warlike character than their neighbours, for they are capable of holding their own against any other tribe, and are spoken of as their equals 'in manliness and spirit.'

They displayed these qualities to good effect during the 'Sikh' domination, and it was said that 'Avitabile,' the savage governor of Peshawur under the 'Sikhs,' whose name is famous or infamous for the ruthless ferocity with which he suppressed revolt, never ventured against the 'Khutuks.' How, then, are we to account for this exceptional character of the tribe, as compared with the representatives of all the other 'Paṭhân' communities along our border? One reason may be, that their country is more open, as a rule, to retaliatory measures. They occupy the hills south of Peshawur to 'Kooshâlgarh' and 'Kâlabâgh' on the Indus, from both of which is a pass to 'Kohât;' and the country has, so to speak, both Kohât and Peshawur in its rear, and part of Kohât and the British district of Bunnoo on its flanks, so that their position is far more exposed than that of the 'Afreedees,' 'Bonairs,' &c.; still that alone would not account for their good behaviour. Another reason is to be found, I think, in their being more under the individual influence of the chief, and less under that of the 'Moolah,' than the other tribes. 'Khooshal Khan' Khutuk was a celebrated chief of this tribe, and in our time 'Khwâja Mahomed Khan' has exercised a most strong influence for good upon the clan. He joined us immediately after the annexation of the province, and adhered to us through good and evil most staunchly. This chief had the farm of the southern portion of the 'Khutuk' hills, and also had charge of the Buhadur Khail salt-mine, both which offices gave him consideration and power among the clan. The 'Khutuks' make excellent soldiers, and many of them are enlisted in our cavalry and infantry regiments.

The next on the roll are the Wuzeerees, who are the pest of the lower, as the 'Afreedees' are of the upper frontier. They are supposed to take their name from one Wuzeer, and are divided into three great branches, named, it is said, after the three sons of Wuzeer—Ahmud-zye, Ootmân-zye, Muhsood.

The 'Ahmudzye' are on the northern, the 'Ootmânzye' on the central, and the 'Muhsoods' on the southern portions of the Bunnoo and Ismail Khan districts, a distance, as the crow flies, of some 120 or 130 miles. Portions of the two first-named branches cultivate land within British territory, and are in a measure pastoral and migratory. The 'Muhsoods' keep to their mountains, and occupy well-built residences. These also, like the other 'Pathân' clans, are subdivided into numerous 'Zyes' and 'Khails.' They number, according to the last estimate, 20,000 fighting men; but this, if the assumed number of the 'Muhsood' section, 12,000, be correct, is probably below the mark. Among the 'Wuzeeree' clans who have given us the most annoyance are the 'Câbul Khail,' of the 'Ootmanzye' branch, bordering the Kohât district, and infesting the valley of 'Meerunzye,' whose inhabitants also have given us much trouble. No less than three military expeditions have been sent to punish these people, and the 'Câbul Khail' have also received three visitations. The occasion of their punishment in 1859-60, was due to their having harboured the assassins of a British officer, Captain Mecham, who was murdered by five men of the 'Hâtee Khail' tribe of the 'Ahmudzye' branch, while journeying from Bunnoo to Kohât. This circumstance is mentioned particularly, as it furnishes one of the very few instances (their number may be counted on the fingers of one hand) of the tribes giving up a malefactor for punishment.

While measures were being taken for the punishment of the 'Cabul Khail,' pressure was brought to bear on the 'Hâtee Khail,' who cultivated a large tract of land in British territory. These possessions of the tribe within our limits, and the fact of their fields being sown at the time, furnished a strong lever by which to work on the self-interests of the tribe, and after some delay and attempts at evasion, which were sternly repressed, the tribe gave up the principal assassin, and he was hanged on the very spot where the crime was committed. The 'Oomurzye' of the 'Ahmudzye' branch gave constant annoyance on the Bunnoo frontier for some time after the establishment of our rule. They also held certain lands within our limits at the time of annexation, but would not conduct themselves as peaceable tillers of the soil.

For three years they kept up a harassing petty warfare on our border, driving off cattle, sometimes attacking and sacking a village, and kidnapping any well-to-do husbandmen they could lay hands on. At last, all measures of conciliation having failed, Major John Nicholson, the Deputy Commissioner of Bunnoo, made a swoop on the tribe with a small force at night—slew some of them, burnt their encampments, and recovered the cattle they had lifted. This movement had all the desired effect. The savage mountaineers were disabused of the idea that their hills were impregnable, and found that they afforded no effective protection against a British force. They made their submission, were re-admitted to a certain extent to their cultivation in British territory, and have behaved with tolerable decency ever since.

The 'Muhsoods' come next under consideration, and with the exception perhaps of the Afreedees, they are the most pestilent and troublesome neighbours we have to deal with along our whole line of frontier. Unlike their fellow-clansmen, they will not take kindly to agricultural pursuits, nor do they carry on the same petty traffic with us in salt, firewood, &c., as do the Afreedees, and which gives us some slight power over that lawless community, by enabling us to close their market when they show themselves hostile. The 'Muhsoods' occupy the mountain range to the south of the Bunnoo, and to the west of the Derah Ismail Khan districts. The range is a vast and lofty one, the principal known hills being the 'Ghubur,' about 7000 feet above the level of the sea; the 'Peerghul,' 11,500; the 'Shuvee Dhur,' 11,000 feet; and behind and above all towers the grand 'Tukht-i-Suleiman' (Throne of Solomon), 14,000 feet above the sea level. The last, however, is, strictly speaking, beyond the 'Muhsood' boundary.

The extent of the line of country they occupy facing our border is about eighty miles as the crow flies, and during the early period of our administration they kept the frontier in constant agitation, driving off cattle at graze near the hills, occasionally attacking the border villages, kidnapping traders, and carrying on a regular system of marauding with comparative impunity. It became necessary to have a chain of fortified posts along the frontier, and to organise a regular system of patrolling between them, but in spite of these measures the 'Muhsoods' continued their raids with unchecked pertinacity for ten years from the time of our becoming their neighbours. We had greater difficulty in dealing with them than with any other of the frontier tribes. There were no means of making reprisals. The 'Muhsoods' had no regular traffic with the plains like the Afreedees; there were no members of the tribe cultivating within our limits, as was the case with the 'Ahmudzye' Wuzeerees; the line of frontier is generally more open to attack opposite the 'Muhsoods' than in other parts, and there is more temptation in the presence of vast numbers of camels belonging to the caravans of 'Powinduh' merchants, which are sent to graze often along the very foot of the hills, on which there are always scouts ready to scent the prey afar off. Then the Muhsoods entertained the idea that they were impregnable in the remote fastnesses of their mountains, and boasted that the foot of an invader had never defiled their native soil, which I believe was true until the military expedition of 1860 dispelled the illusion as to their impregnability.

In March 1860, incited thereto probably by long years of forbearance on our part, they made a hostile demonstration on the town of 'Tâk,' some four or five miles from the frontier line, and came on about 4000 strong with the intention of sacking the town. To meet them there were only about 160 sabres of the 5th Punjaub cavalry and some police troopers, under the command of a native officer of the 5th named 'Sahâdut Khan,' a resolute soldier, and, as he proved himself, a good tactician. Drawing out his small body of cavalry, he advanced to meet the 'Muhsood' invaders, but suddenly, terrified as it appeared to them, by their imposing array, he commenced a retrograde movement. The 'Muhsoods' followed helter-skelter, firing their matchlocks, and showering abuse on the fugitives' heads, when, having obtained his object in drawing the 'Muhsoods' clear of the hill ravines, and into the open, where cavalry could act, he wheeled his small troop about, and charged down on the disorganised body of the enemy.

A complete rout was the result, numbers were slain and wounded, and the whole rabble made off to the hills as fast as their mountain legs would carry them. Their loss was 200 killed and a large number wounded. On our side there were one trooper killed and fifteen

EXPEDITION AGAINST THE 'MUHSOODS.' 73

wounded, and several horses killed and wounded. This unprovoked aggression of the 'Muhsoods' was the filling of the cup, and the Government at last consented to a military expedition against them. About the middle of April, General Chamberlain marched with about 5000 native troops, including two field batteries and two mountain trains of artillery, to explore the fastnesses of the 'Peerghul,' and to exact retribution from the 'Muhsoods' at their very doors for the long course of provocation and injury we had endured at their hands.

This expedition against the 'Muhsoods' is, it is believed, unique in the history of our military operations against the tribes, and may call for a more extended notice. On other occasions we have either adhered to our base, as at Umbelah, effected the punishment of the offenders by a rapid night march, surprising them in their homes, as in the expedition against the 'Oomurzye' above alluded to, and in that against the 'Buzotis' conducted by General Keyes, or the nature of the ground has enabled us to conduct our offensive movements without fear of our communications being cut off, as in the expeditions against the 'Meerunzye' valley. But in this case the General cast to the winds all considerations of keeping open our communications, and, confident in his own powers of command and the excellence of his troops, threw himself boldly into the middle of the enemy's country, leaving the communications to care for themselves. It was a bold, perhaps a hazardous step, but the result justified the General's confidence in all particulars.

CHAPTER VII.

Campaign against the Muhsoods—Its results—The Butunnees—Sheoranees—Oosterânees—The Powinduh merchants—The Bilooch tribes — Their character as compared with the Pathâns — The Scinde frontier — The Punjaub frontier force.

THE force marched from 'Tâk' about the middle of April. The route lay for the earlier part of the march up the bed of the 'Zâm' river or stream, which takes its rise in the 'Peerghul' mountain, and forms a kind of main artery to the country, affording irrigation to their scanty area of corn cultivation. The channels for supplying water to the fields from this source were very creditable samples of savage engineering. They were often found cut along the side of a rock for long distances, and sometimes where the rock was altogether impracticable, the water was carried through tunnels.

The stony course of the 'Zâm' afforded rather a rough pathway, but the troops marched merrily along it, and the field guns travelled without much difficulty. The mountain guns of course were carried on mules. At this time of the year (spring) the stream of the 'Zam' is scanty and shallow, probably not more than two or three feet deep, but in the rainy season and after the melting of the snow, it becomes a turbid torrent often impassable. The first brush with the enemy was at 'Kot Shingee,' an important village, to surprise which a night march was effected; but the 'Muhsoods' evacuated the place, and only tried some long shots from the hills above. Here was seen the singular spectacle of cavalry skirmishing up a mountain-side. A troop of the Guides followed the retreating enemy some way up the hills, exchanging shots with them, and capturing a flock of some 150 sheep and goats from them, a welcome addition to the commissariat.

The force then moved on, still up the bed of the 'Zâm,' to 'Puloseen,' whence General Chamberlain marched with 3000 men to threaten or disperse a gathering of the tribe at 'Shuhoor,' leaving Colonel Lumsden in command at 'Puloseen' with about 1500 men. Here the 'Muhsoods' gave us a Rowland for our Oliver, and requited the attack on 'Kot Shingee' by a similar surprise on our camp. They selected the morning of the 'Eed,' the great religious festival of the Mohammedans (on the principle of the better day the better deed), for their attempt, and, which seemed to show that they had some trained soldiers among them, as had been surmised, they chose the time of withdrawing the piquets at daybreak to make their 'hooroosh' on the camp. They managed to surprise the piquets as they were about to fall in and move off, and the camp was awakened by the sounds, almost simultaneous, of the *reveille* and the ping of the 'Muhsood' bullets. For about ten minutes there was a good deal of confusion, and if the 'Muhsoods' had only known how to keep together and make a combined rush, they might have made the matter serious, but directly they were past the piquets they came in, each man for himself, dancing about, and slashing right and left with their heavy swords, without any definite aim or purpose. Discipline soon asserted itself, and the 'Muhsoods' were speedily driven out of camp, leaving 130 of their party dead, and a large number wounded. The other portion of the force rejoined two days after, and the camp halted to allow of the sick and wounded being sent into the plains.

On the 1st May the 'jirgah' of the 'Muhsoods' came in for a conference. Our object was fully explained to them. We had put up with unnumbered affronts and injuries from the tribe for the last ten years, and we had now come to exact redress for the past and guarantees for the future, the former to consist of a fine of £1400, the latter that hostages were to be furnished for the good behaviour of the tribe in future. After a long palaver the 'jirgah' declared their inability to accede to the terms, and were dismissed with the intimation that the force would march through their country to 'Kâneegoorum,' the 'Muhsood' capital, and repeat the terms there. If unmolested, the march would be conducted peaceably on our part, but if attacked, the 'Muhsoods' must abide by the consequences. After a day or two's halt to make the necessary preparations, and to send all the sick and wounded into the plains—for from this point there could be no further communication with the rear—the force continued its march, still keeping to the bed of the 'Zâm.' Though flanked generally by rugged hillsides, there were every now and then some lovely spots near the bed of the stream, elbows and corners where in former years the torrents had deposited alluvial soil, and upon which had sprung up poplar and willow saplings, now grown into large and shapely trees, while the green sward beneath helped to make up a small oasis, amid the sterile surroundings of the stony bed of the 'Zâm' and the rocky cliffs above. It soon became evident that the 'Muhsoods' intended to try an appeal to arms to prevent the threatened march on their capital, and on the third day after the 'jirgah' had left camp, they were found in considerable strength, occupying a position selected with much military skill and judgment.

Across the bed of the 'Zâm,' which here ran through a narrow gorge, with rugged and lofty hills on either side, they had constructed a most formidable *abattis*, made of huge boulders with trunks and large branches of trees interwoven with them, with the branches protruding from the front like a *chevaux de frise*. On the heights on either side they had piled up strong stone breastworks to prevent their flank being turned, and they held both the centre and flanking positions in very considerable force. It was necessary of course to capture the heights before advancing to attack the *abattis* in the gorge, and a brigade with mountain train attached was sent up on each side for that purpose. The right attack was perhaps the most difficult, as the ascent was steeper than on the left, and the summit of the hill on which the strongest breastwork was constructed was more precipitous. A temporary check occurred here, which might have had serious consequences. The leading regiment, on arriving just below the point where the upper breastwork was, were in rather scattered order, and blown with the stiffness of the ascent, which the enemy observing, made a rush upon them with all the impetus of a down-hill charge, and drove them and the regiment in support back on the reserve, where however the 'Muhsoods' were met with a rattling discharge from the mountain guns, and by a counter charge from the 1st Punjaub infantry, which not only checked their rush, but drove them back, and our troops following them up at once, a headlong flight was the result.

Meanwhile the attack on the left position had been progressing steadily under cover of the fire from the mountain guns, and when the defenders of the breastworks on that side saw the result of the right attack, they also took to their heels, as did the garrison of the *abattis*. Our troops followed the fugitives for some distance, but the light-footed mountaineers soon outstripped our more heavily weighted infantry, and dispersed after their usual fashion to their homes. These mountain hosts can only be kept together for a few days at a time, as their commissariat is represented by what each man carries for himself, probably a supply for five days or a week. When that is expended, he must go home to recruit his store, as his leaders have none to give him, and the neighbouring villages have none to spare, so that those that come from a distance to join the gathering, have to reckon not only for the period in which they may be actively engaged, but for their journey out and home. Here Robertson's description of the American warriors may again be quoted: —'Their armies are not encumbered with baggage or military stores. Each warrior, besides his arms, carries a mat and a small bag of pounded maize, and with these is completely equipped for any service' (Hist. Amer., vol. ii. p. 153). This is an exact description of Wuzeeree habits, even to the character of provender carried, which generally consists of ground Indian-corn. After their second defeat the 'Muhsoods' did not again make head to oppose the onward march of the British force, which was a matter of surprise to most of the officers, as the Muhsoods were considered the most united clan on the border, but they had suffered heavily, both at 'Puloseen' and in the second fight, and having no leader and no commissariat, their collapse was complete for the time.

Our force marched on without opposition to the Muhsood capital, 'Kâneegoorum,' described as 'picturesquely built on a succession of shelves. The valley below on either side very pretty. Trees and cultivation in abundance.' The inhabitants came out to meet the force, and tendered their submission, and the town was spared. The troops then moved on to 'Mukeen,' a populous village, or rather cluster of villages. This was burnt, the inhabitants not having come to terms, and the force then marched through the country, skirting the lofty 'Peerghul' mountain, and debouching opposite Bunnoo, having been just a fortnight in a thoroughly hostile mountain country, without any communication with the plains, and with no supplies but those carried with the troops. Considering the nature of the country to be traversed, and the fierce character of the tribe we had to deal with, it must be allowed, that the exploit reflects the highest credit both on the General and the troops. The expedition had the result of keeping the 'Muhsoods' quiet for a time, and they have never again attempted a hostile demonstration in force, but they are not yet cured of marauding, and an attempt to induce them to colonise in British territory, though it looked hopeful at one time, has not as yet turned out a success. The Umbelah and 'Muhsood' expeditions have been discussed at some length, as illustrating operations of an entirely opposite character, but the reader shall not be troubled with any more campaigns.

The 'Buttunees' come next in order—a small and insignificant tribe, which occupies the slopes of the 'Ghubur' hill, and a portion of the country between the 'Tâk' district and the 'Muhsoods.' They can muster three or four thousand matchlocks, but they are in no way formidable in the field. They play the jackal between the 'Muhsoods' and the 'Tak' people, and are sometimes mischievous in that way. They hold lands to some extent within our border.

The Pathân clan next in order to the above are the 'Sheoranees.'

These, like the Muhsoods, are a thieving, marauding lot, but they have neither the strength nor the unity of the Muhsoods, nor is their country so difficult of access. They inhabit the mountain border of the Derah Ismail

Khan district, and number perhaps 6000 fighting men. In the early part of our occupation they gave a good deal of trouble, and in 1853 an expedition was organised against them. A force of about 2400 men under General Hodgson marched into their country, remained there three or four days, and burnt their chief town, 'Koteli,' and many of their fortified villages. This lesson had a good effect, and the 'Sheoranees' have continued pretty quiet ever since. The last Pathân tribe are the Oosterânees, a small but gallant body, who occupy some of the spurs of the Suleimâni range, and who cultivate to a certain extent along the foot of the hills. They have not given us much annoyance by acts of offence against ourselves, but they were constantly at feud with their Bilooch neighbours, the 'Kusrânees,' in the course of which our border was often made the cockpit of the rival clans. Matters are quieter now, and we have no reason to complain of the 'Oosterânees' as neighbours.

Before taking our leave of the Pathân tribes, mention should be made of the 'Powindahs,' as they are called, a body of travelling merchants, who bring the produce of Affghanistan, Bokhara, &c., to India. They travel with 'kâfilahs,' or caravans as they are termed in English, though that interpretation hardly represents the equivalent of the Arabic word. These 'kâfilahs' consist sometimes of several hundred camels, laden with woollen stuffs, Cabul grapes, madder, sheepskin coats and cloaks, woollen socks and other apparel, pistachio nuts, dried fruits, and Persian cats; others bring horses only. From near Ghuznee, in Affghanistan, to the Derah Ismail Khan frontier, which they enter by the 'Goomul' and other small passes, the 'Powindah' merchants often have to fight their way throughout the greater part of the distance, or at all events, in those parts which bring them into contact with the Muhsood and other Wuzeeree clans. But these warrior-traders generally manage to run the gauntlet with comparative immunity from loss as regards their merchandise, though they suffer occasionally in person from the swords and matchlocks of the 'Muhsood' robbers. There is, it is probable, some kind of agreement in the shape of blackmail between the 'Powindahs' and the Muhsoods, but, as before noticed, the members of these savage tribes often run counter to the views of their head men, and hence the not unfrequent assaults on the 'Powindah' kâfilahs by isolated bodies to satisfy their private greed. The 'Powindahs,' on arriving in the plains, readjust their camels' loads, so as to leave the weaker animals and those with young to graze during the winter months in the Derah districts, and move on with the rest to the nearest point on the Lahore and Mooltan Railway. In former times they marched on bodily with their camels to Delhi, Agra, and Calcutta, the last-named place being some twelve or thirteen hundred miles from their point of departure at Derah Ismail Khan. After disposing of their merchandise, and reloading their camels with European and Indian goods, they return to their encampments in time to move off on their homeward route before the hot weather sets in. While those who proceed down-country with the goods are absent, the members of the party who remain to look after the camels occupy encampments in front of the frontier hills. These encampments are made up of small black camel-hair tents, and are called 'Kirrees,'—'kirree' meaning black. The camels are allowed to graze sometimes on the slopes of the hills, and this occasionally brings on a collision between the 'Wuzeerees' and 'Powindahs,' the former, as noticed above, 'lifting' the 'Powindahs'' camels when they get a chance, and the latter, pursuing the raiders into the hills, often recover their property and punish the Wuzeerees into the bargain. This summary method, however, is not allowed by the Government, and the 'Powindahs' have been obliged to make reparation occasionally for the punishment inflicted on the Wuzeeree robbers, who, it need hardly be said, richly deserved it. The 'Powindahs' are divided into clans like the rest of the Affghans. The best known are the 'Nâsirs' and 'Meean Khail.' With the exception of one small tribe, this completes the catalogue of the Pathân tribes on the frontier.

The Bilooches join the Pathâns at the southern extremity of the Derah Ismail Khan district. The next tribe to the Pathâns is the 'Kusrânees,' who were always squabbling with the 'Oosterânees,' as noticed above, and who harassed our frontier a good deal during the early part of our rule. They were punished by the same expedition which visited the 'Sheoranees' in 1853, and they have been better neighbours since. They number perhaps 3000 or 4000 fighting men. Next to the 'Kusrânees' come the 'Bôzdârs,' about 4000 strong. These also were troublesome for some years, but in 1857 they were punished by a force under General

Chamberlain, the troops returning to quarters just in time to march off to Delhi on the outbreak of the Mutiny. This punishment of the 'Bôzdârs' had a good effect in keeping that part of the border quiet during the throes of the Mutiny, and the 'Bôzdârs' themselves have conducted themselves respectably since. Of course, in stating that tribes have become better neighbours, the commendation is only comparative. Cattle-lifting and robbery still go on more or less, but the better-disposed clans abstain from violence as a rule, and from actively offensive measures.

Next to the 'Bôzdârs' comes a small Pathân tribe called 'Khetrâns,' who are curiously sandwiched among the 'Biloochees.' They are or were troublesome, rather on account of their feuds with their Bilooch neighbours beyond the frontier, than for hostile acts within our border. After the Khetrâns follow Kosahs, Lughârees, Gurchânees, Murrees, and Boogtees, occupying the frontier line of the Dera Ghazi Khan district, down to its point of junction with the Scinde border. These number probably 12,000 or 15,000 fighting men, but they have not given us nearly so much trouble as the Pathâns. As a rule, their country is more accessible than the rugged cliffs and difficult passes in the Pathân mountains, and the people themselves are more manageable. They are neither so bigoted nor so obstinate as the Affghan people. They have less respect for the Moolah, and more for the chief, to which latter the Bilooch tribes on the Punjaub frontier render, as a rule, a fair quota of obedience, and hence it is easier to deal with them than with communities represented by such feeble and vacillating agents as the Pathân 'jirgahs.' The province of Scinde meets the Punjaub at 'Kusmore.' Its frontier posts cover about 190 miles, but they are a long way from the hills. The tribes on the Scinde frontier are the Murrees and Boogtees noticed above, the Doomkees, Jikranees, Ramdanees, Kosahs, Boordees, Muzzârees and others, the last six named being inhabitants of the Cuchee and Scinde plains. The Scinde frontier is or was watched entirely by cavalry, their posts being some fifty or sixty miles from the hills, except at the two extremities. The force consists of two regiments of Scinde Horse, numbering altogether 1600 sabres. There will be occasion to offer some remarks hereafter on the respective characteristics of the Scinde and Punjaub systems of frontier management. Having enumerated the Pathân tribes which march with our border, and having noticed the system of depredation and onslaughts on our frontier villages and subjects so persistently carried on by them, it will be desirable, perhaps, to say a few words regarding the force by which this long extent of frontier is to be watched and protected.

Peshawur, the most important station, as commanding the principal route from Cabul *viâ* the Khyber Pass, is garrisoned by the regular army. The force consists of two European infantry regiments, two native cavalry regiments, four or five native infantry regiments, and three or four batteries of artillery. There is a reserve at 'Noshera' about twenty miles from Peshawur, half way between it and the Indus, consisting of one European and one native infantry regiment and one regiment of native cavalry. The Peshawur brigade furnishes detachments to garrison the outposts of 'Michnee,' 'Abozye,' and 'Shubkuddar,' facing the 'Momunds,' and Fort Mackeson observing the Kohât Pass. The cantonment of Peshawur is opposite to, and about four miles from, the mouth of the Khyber Pass. In any military operations having for their object the punishment of the 'Momunds,' of the Afreedees of the Khyber, and of the northern face of the Kohât Pass, the force would be furnished by the Peshawur brigade; all other frontier expeditions are, as a rule, conducted by the Punjaub frontier force. This force is constituted as follows:—Two field batteries and two mountain trains, six regiments of cavalry, including the Guides, numbering about 2500 sabres, and twelve regiments of infantry, mustering 7640 rank and file, or, including non-commissioned officers, about 11,000 men. They are distributed as follows:—Two infantry regiments and a mountain battery in 'Huzârah.' The Guides, consisting of one cavalry and one infantry regiment, garrison 'Yusufzye.' At Kohât are three regiments of infantry, a regiment of cavalry, a mountain battery, and a garrison company of artillery. At Bunnoo, two regiments of infantry, one of cavalry, and a field battery. At Derah Ismail Khan the same detail, with the addition of a detachment of European infantry which garrisons the fort. At Derah Ghazi Khan are two regiments of infantry and one of cavalry, and at Rajunpore, the southernmost station in the province, and near the Scinde border, is one regiment of cavalry. This force supplies detachments to garrison the outposts, extending over 500 miles of

THE PUNJAUB FRONTIER FORCE.

frontier, and furnishes when necessary the means for punishing the frontier tribes, keeping up a regular establishment of mules in each regiment to enable them to move at a moment's notice. There is no relief from outpost duty. Unlike regiments in the quieter and more central portions of the province, who only have to furnish the regimental and station guards, and get four nights in out of five, the Punjaub force, as a rule, is never off duty, having, in addition to the ordinary guards, to supply the outposts as well. During the twenty-eight years of our occupation of the Punjaub, there have been about thirty military expeditions against the frontier tribes, in all of which, with perhaps the exception of two or three against the 'Momunds,' the Punjaub frontier force has been engaged. Numberless reports have told of the gallant work they have done, but few of these unfortunately have come to public notice, in consequence of most of the warlike operations in which the Punjaub frontier force has been engaged having been conducted under the orders of the Civil Government, and not under the Commander-in-chief. The despatches, however, published during the Umbelah campaign teem with commendations of their gallantry; and no one will deny that the men of the Punjaub frontier force are second to none in the qualities that constitute a soldier, and that in the matter of warlike experience they are superior to most, as having been constantly under arms since the annexation of the Punjaub.

And what has been their reward? Echo replies, like an Irishman, with the question. Reward? With the single exception of the general commanding, there is not, it is believed, a single officer in the whole eighteen regiments and four batteries of artillery who can write C.B. after his name. Considering the manner in which honours were showered after the Abyssinian and Ashantee campaigns, one is struck with amazement that the gallant body of men in the Punjaub force should have been so long neglected. No soldier would be so invidious as to detract from the merit due to one brave man to glorify another, but it might be fairly asserted that the honours awarded for Abyssinia and Ashantee have been earned by the officers of the Punjaub force twice over. The only way in which to account for the treatment they have received is, that being a civil corps, that is, under the orders of the local government, and not under the military chief, the officers' claims have not been brought to notice with sufficient earnestness, or the very fact of their not being under the military authorities may tell against them. Whatever the cause, the result is injustice; and it is not to be wondered at that the officers of the Punjaub force desire to change masters. The subject of placing the frontier force under the Commander-in-chief, has been under consideration for many years past, but it has not been effected up to the present time. There are strong arguments, certainly, on the side of its being maintained as a local force. The advantage derived from the officers knowing the country and the character of the tribes we have to deal with, which could not be attained in the ordinary course of service, where corps are relieved every two or three years, the facility of obtaining recruits from among the

Pathâns, which would not be the case if regiments were liable to be marched to distant stations down-country, as the Pathâns suffer from home-sickness to a considerable extent;—these and other circumstances are in favour of the frontier force being continued as a local body. But, on the other hand, the fact of a large body of troops, equal to two divisions, occupying the most important position in India, being independent of the Commander-in-chief in India, and in no way subject to his control, carries such an anomaly on the very face of it, as to outweigh the considerations advanced in favour of the localisation of the force. Add to this, that under present circumstances the officers and men have much harder work than their brethren in the more settled parts of the country, and that their services never meet with acknowledgment, and it must be allowed, I think, that, from the military point of view, the arguments for the assimilation of the frontier force to the rest of the army in India are overpowering. It may be noted here, that when officers of the Punjaub force have come under the orders of the Commander-in-chief, their services have met with prompt recognition. Thus Wilde, Green, Hughes, Browne, Probyn, and Watson, who were all in the frontier force, and who marched down with their regiments, or portions of them, to join the army before Delhi during the Mutiny of 1857, all received their C.B.'s and three of them the Victoria Cross. It may be replied that the work of that time was exceptional both in severity of fighting and stress of climate; but that surely cannot be urged with reference to Abyssinia and Ashantee; and if twenty or twenty-five years' work on a hostile frontier (and many of the Punjaub officers can show so much), under the conditions above described, does not entitle a soldier to the rewards accorded for military service, it is difficult to know what is the necessary qualification.

Part II.

CHAPTER VIII.

Characteristics of the border tribes—Their religion—Blood-feuds—Theft—Treatment of women—Social customs—Hypothesis of the Affghâns being the lost Ten Tribes of Israel—The 'Vesh'—Similarity of this custom to Jewish institutions—Arms of the Affghâns—Military system—Treachery of the Affghâns—Strength of the different tribes.

BEFORE considering the different systems of frontier management, it is proposed to offer a few remarks on the characteristics of the frontier tribes, and first as to their religion. They are Mohammedans, 'Soonees,'[1] without exception, and a 'Sheeah' would be likely to have a bad time of it amongst them. They are strict in the observance of the times of prayer, the ceremonial ablutions, and of the fasts and festivals of their creed.

---

[1] 'Soonee,' lit. 'lawful,' one who reveres equally the four successors of Mohammed. 'Sheeah,' a follower of 'Ali,' Mohammed's son-in-law. The Turks are 'Soonees,' the Persians 'Sheeahs.'

They are given, too, to honouring the shrines of departed saints, they make pilgrimages to them, and decorate their tombs with lamps and flowers on anniversaries and festivals. It is, therefore, a feather in the cap of a tribe to be possessed of a shrine of special sanctity. An amusing story is told of one of the wild tribes adjoining the 'Khyber,' with reference to this amiable weakness.

It happened that the tribe in question was unfortunate in having no 'remains' of sufficient sanctity to do pilgrimage to, and they were twitted in consequence by the neighbouring tribes on their spiritual destitution. It so fell out that a 'Moolah,' or learned priest of some reputed sanctity, came to their village on his way elsewhere. He was received with much honour, and all the rites of hospitality were duly accorded, when, unfortunately for him, it occurred to the heads of the community that this was a grand opportunity for providing themselves with a 'Zeeârut,' or place of pilgrimage; so they killed the unfortunate priest, and inducted his remains into the place of honour forthwith, setting themselves free from the sneers of their neighbours by this primitive proceeding.

But ignorance goes hand-in-hand with their bigotry. The Pathân Pharisee, who recites his five prayers a day, who will fast religiously from sunrise to sunset during the whole month of the Ramzân, the Mohammedan Lent, not allowing even water to pass his lips during that interval, and who would cut your or his own throat at the mere sign of his spiritual adviser, is as ignorant as the swine he professes to abominate.

He cannot render you a reason for the faith which is in him. What is, is; what must be, must be, is the beginning, middle, and ending of his creed. He can repeat the 'Kulmah,' or profession of faith, 'There is one Allah, and Mohammed is the prophet of Allah,' and gabble through his five appointed prayer-times, and do this with just as much unction and devotion when he is on his way to rob a neighbour or commit a murder, as if he was about to be engaged in a righteous and meritorious action; so that it may be presumed that all this external devotion exercises no influence whatever on the life of a Pathân Mohammedan. So long as he pays to Allah what he considers his due in the way of prayers, ablutions, &c., well, but in all other matters he is his own master. It may be thought that this is an exaggerated picture, but there are good grounds for the belief that the idea of doing right because it is right does not enter into a Pathân's philosophy; that murder, theft, and adultery are only abstained from according to the degree of fear which is entertained of retribution, and not from any respect for the property or life of man or the honour of woman. There is no fear of law, for, as has been said above, the first step towards a regular jurisdiction has not been taken in these rude societies. Murder, in the course of a blood-feud, is a righteous act; not in fair and open fight, but by midnight assassination, or by a safe shot from behind a rock; for if the avenger were to get the worst of it in the attempt, the other party would score two! The debtor and creditor account of blood is most religiously kept, and murder follows murder with arithmetical precision. This may be illustrated by an anecdote of which 'Sher Ali,' the man who subsequently assassinated Lord Mayo, is the subject. He was a member of one of the clans in the vicinity of the Khyber Pass, and while he was mounted orderly to the Commissioner of Peshawur, he used to get leave from that officer to go home for a week or so, borrowing or begging at the same time some powder and lead. He returned after one of these excursions, and announced that he had arranged his matters satisfactorily, which arrangement consisted in shooting his uncle or cousin, with whom he was at feud. It was for decoying another person with whom he had a difference, and effecting his murder on British territory, that 'Sher Ali' received the sentence of banishment to the 'Andamans,' where he consummated his crimes by the murder of Lord Mayo.

In the matter of theft, expertness and skill in the art of robbing are praiseworthy qualities in the eyes of many Pathán tribes. In one of the clans near Peshawur, there is a custom for infants to be passed through a hole dug in the wall as by a burglar, the parents at the same time repeating the words, 'Ghul shé, ghul shé,' 'Be a thief, be a thief,' which is a *baptême de vole* with a witness. But there are degrees of baseness even among thieves. The tribes opposite Peshawur and bordering on the 'Khyber Pass' are perhaps the worst in this particular. 'Shinwárees,' 'Moolagorees,' 'Zukakhail,' and some of the 'Afreedees' near the Kohat Pass, bear an infamous character, as do the lower 'Wuzeerees.'

It may be desirable to notice now the subject of

Pathán women in reference to their social position. Generally they are treated as Mohammedan women are in other localities. Unrespected, distrusted, the drudges of the household, and objects of a brute sensuality, describe pretty well the position of Pathán women. Degraded by treatment like this, it is hardly to be expected that any of the feminine virtues and excellences which distinguish the sex in our own happy land should be developed by these unhappy creatures, and it must almost follow, as the night the day, that their minds should be depraved, and that anything like loyalty or affection towards their lords and masters are qualities not to be looked for in them. The consequence is that conjugal infidelity is common, and this is often followed by the murder both of the woman and her paramour, which, of course, originates a blood-feud, and so the game goes on.

It is almost a foregone conclusion in taking up an inquiry into a murder among Pathans, that 'a woman is at the bottom of it.' The Pathán women are often attractive in appearance, but have little sensibility and less intellect.

They are never allowed to join the men in any of their social gatherings. They fetch the water, do the cooking, look after the house, and so forth, but their social enjoyments are confined to gossiping and quarrelling among themselves. They have not even the gratification which the more favoured women in Hindostan enjoy of counting over their clothes and ornaments. A Pathán female's wardrobe and jewel-box would be represented by a very small total. A blue upper garment and trousers to match would probably complete the list of her habiliments, and a silver armlet or two, and possibly an anklet of the same metal, would sum up the amount of her finery. Such being the condition of the women, and the character of the male portion of the community such as has been described above, the country they inhabit rugged and unproductive, no commerce to bring the people into contact with other races, no system of government to assist social and political development, it is hardly to be wondered at that the Pathâns have not yet issued from the savage state, nor until there is a stable and enlightened Government at Cabul to exercise pressure on them from that quarter, and to co-operate with our efforts on the east of Affghanistan, does there seem to be the slightest probability of their emerging from this barbarous condition. 'Tis pity, too, for physically they are a fine people, and they possess also some of the best qualities of the savage—bravery, hospitality, and, among themselves, fidelity to their salt. That they have the making of good men in them is evident from the numerous samples we have in the Punjaub frontier force. Some of the regiments are largely recruited from the Pathâns of the border, notably the Guides and the 1st Punjaub Infantry; and the faithful service these men have done at Delhi, Lucknow, in numberless border expeditions, and especially at Umbelah, where they were in arms against their own spiritual pastor, deserves to be written in letters of gold. It would seem that there must have been some mistake in our mode of dealing with the tribes hitherto, or, with such good material to be met with, we should have made a nearer approach to a good understanding with them, a point that will be noticed further when treating of frontier management.

Among the social customs of the Pathâns may be mentioned the practice among some tribes of assembling together in the evening at a place set apart for the purpose to smoke their pipes and discuss village affairs, the women of course not being admitted. This rendezvous is called in some parts the 'Chouk,' but more generally among Pathâns the 'Hoojra.' Here the villagers congregate after the day's work is over for society and conversation, and often keep up the 'sederunt' till after midnight. When there are two parties in a village, each has its separate club, the partisans of each adhering religiously to their own assembly.

The spot selected for the 'Hoojra' is generally the foot of a large tree near the centre of the village, with water at hand for ceremonial ablutions and other purposes. The 'Hoojra' is the place allotted for the reception and entertainment of travellers, who are provided for by a general subscription of bread, &c., from the habitués of the club. A regular servant is kept for the 'Hoojra,' often a 'meerâsi' or musician, who entertains the evening assemblies with music. Besides this, his duties are to keep the 'Hoojra' clean, wait upon travellers, fill the visitors' pipes, &c. He is remunerated by a certain allowance of grain at each harvest, and he also receives a small fee on each occasion of a wedding in the village.

The police organisation of a Pathân community is, as has been above intimated, of the weakest order, but one institution may be noticed, which is good in intention, if not always successful in practice. On the occurrence of any robbery or act of violence in a village, all the abled-bodied portion of the community are expected to turn out in pursuit of the offenders. This is called the 'chigheh,' the English equivalent of which probably would be 'hue and cry.' The success of the system depends of course on the promptness with which the summons to turn out is obeyed.

Only a glance can be given at the interesting hypothesis of the Affghans being the lost Ten Tribes. This has been fully discussed by more than one writer, notably by Sir George Rose.

The similarity of feature in the Affghan and the Jew is often striking, and the division of the people into tribes bearing familiar Scripture names, as Ishmael, Esau, David, Joseph, &c., might be accepted, among other incidents, as indications of Israelitish descent. The practice of avenging blood is common to the Jews and the Pathâns, but it is found also among other Eastern nations, and cannot therefore be included in the category of exceptional coincidences. The most singular instance of resemblance, as far as customs are concerned, is the transfer of property among the Pathâns known by the term 'vesh.' After the lapse of several years, the members of a tribe will change possessions bodily. So far as our recollection goes, no exact term is fixed, but after thirty or forty years, perhaps less, there will be a general move and redistribution of the land by lot, A moving into B's estate, B into C's perhaps, and C again into A's, and this without

PATHÁN LANGUAGE. 99

any payment or compensation. Unless the Affghans derived this peculiar practice from the jubilee of Israel, or from the division of the land by lot, perhaps from an amalgamation of the two, it is difficult to conceive how they came by it. The 'vesh' is not carried out with the regularity observed in the jubilee, nor does the Affghan necessarily return to the estate he held at the previous 'vesh,' but still the practice is so singular, so peculiar to Pathán tribes, and bears, at all events in its general principles, so near a resemblance to the Hebrew customs, that we may look upon it as a strong point at least in favour of those who hold the hypothesis of which we have been speaking. It is stated also that the Affghans term themselves 'Ben-i-Israel,'—sons of Israel,—and even that they derive their name from Affghana, a son of Saul, king of Israel. Enough has been advanced, however, by the advocates for the identity of the Affghans with the lost tribes to show that the subject is a very interesting one, and to demonstrate that the claims of the Affghans to be the representatives of Israel are superior to those of the many candidates who have been named for this honour.

The author is not philologist enough to offer any opinion on the language spoken by the Pathâns, known amongst us as 'Pushtoo,' but pronounced by themselves 'Pukhtoo,' with the guttural 'kh.' Some contend that it is a Semitic language, others that it is of Sanscrit origin, and others, again, that it is an independent tongue. There are many Persian and Arabic words to be found in Pukhtoo as well as Sanscrit, and numberless others not traceable to either language; so there is plenty of room for controversy as to whether 'Pukhtoo' is a debased form of Arabic or of Sanscrit, or if it can claim to be an original tongue. There is not, it is believed, much diversity of dialect among the Pathân tribes.

The arms used by the Pathâns are the matchlock, sword, knife or dagger, and occasionally the pistol, and a shield for purposes of defence. The matchlock varies in size and weight, but the make is similar in all sizes. The stock is short and sometimes crooked, the Pathân elevating the elbow, instead of depressing it, as we do in taking aim. The barrel varies from three and a half to nearly five feet in length, and the butt runs up to within a short space of the muzzle, as in the old 'Brown Bess.' The lighter matchlock is carried in a sling across the back or on the shoulder, and aim is taken from the shoulder, standing, sitting, or reclining. The heavier weapon has a fork attached to it, on which the barrel rests while taking aim. The ammunition consists of very coarse-grained powder, and balls, often of hammered iron. The piece is discharged by a cotton match. Flint and steel guns are also met with occasionally, and in the neighbourhood of Peshawur an armoury of English weapons might possibly be found among the tribes near that station, the result of many successful forays. The 'Khyber' Pass robbers have done a good deal of business in this line. On one occasion two of them carried off all the arms of an European guard, including the sentry's. The men were sleeping in the guardhouse with their weapons, carbines and swords, lying by them. The sentry was on his beat outside with a sword. For some reason or other he placed his sword against the wall of the guardhouse, and in the brief interval that his attention was diverted, the whole of the arms of the guard, including the sentry's sword, were carried off. Many stories are current of the expertness of these hill robbers, especially in abstracting horses.

Some of the Pathân matchlocks will carry a long distance, do mischief probably at three or four hundred yards; and where an attack is to be made on them in position, the weapon is a dangerous one; but in the open, from the time it takes to load, and the necessity of perfect stillness to ensure anything like accuracy of aim, it is an arm very little to be dreaded. The Pathân sword is a heavy curved weapon, of inferior metal, but deadly at close quarters from its weight and sharpness. No Pathân, and indeed, as a rule, no Oriental swordsman, ever thinks of making a thrust. It is all cut and slash with them, and they know little or nothing of the parry.

The Affghan knife is a murderous weapon, heavy in blade and handle, like an exaggerated butcher's knife. A dagger also is frequently carried, the blade of which is from nine inches to a foot long, double edged, and thicker sometimes near the point than at the handle. The handle is formed by two parallel steel bars, with a transverse one in the centre for the grip. The parallel bars are eight or nine inches in length, and strong enough to protect the wrist and lower part of the arm from a sword-cut.

The Pathâns have no artillery among the mountain

tribes, neither have the latter any semblance of military tactics or drill, though the troops of the Ameer of 'Câbul' pretend to a regular system. The great object among all 'Pathâns' is to surprise their enemy, and there are no high-flown ideas of chivalry or generosity which interfere with their taking advantage of any means, worthy or unworthy, to attain his discomfiture. We had a sample of this in the massacre of our troops in Affghanistan in 1841, when the Affghan chiefs, with Akhbar Khan, the heir to the throne, at their head, foully broke their faith. Macnaghten was murdered by Akhbar Khan himself, after having come, at that chief's own invitation, to a friendly conference. The remains of the British force, which marched from 'Câbul' under the assurance of safe-conduct from the same individual, were slaughtered to a man, literally, Dr. Brydon being the sole survivor of the force who reached 'Jellalabad.' If this were the case with the 'Câbul' Affghans, who pretend to a higher degree of civilisation, under the command of a single ruler, and seeing that the heir to the throne himself was the instigator and principal actor in this diabolical treachery, what is to be expected from Pathâns of a ruder order, and under no control of either king or chief?

It may be interesting to show the estimated strength of the several tribes. One list is taken from an early report of the Punjaub Administration, the other from a report of later date:—

NUMBERS OF THE TRIBES.

	Report of 1849-51.	Report of 1869-70.
Afreedees	15,000	20,000
Orukzyes	...	30,000
Black Mountain tribes	6,000	8,000
Momunds	12,000	12,000
Khutuks	15,000	...
Yusufzyes	30,000	...
Swatees	...	20,000
Wuzeerees	15,000	20,000
Kusrânees	5,000	...
Bozdârs	...	5,000
Buttunees	5,000	...
Bilooches	25,000	15,000
	128,000	130,000

A subsequent account rates the numbers of the tribes at 170,000.

It will be seen that the two first lists, though varying in details, correspond nearly in their general results. The later estimate, which gives a large increase on the other two, is most likely to be the true one; but it must be remembered that, under no possible contingency, could we expect to have the entire strength of the tribes arrayed against us. It would be impossible, for instance, for the 'Muhsood' 'Wuzeerees' to send a contingent to help the 'Momunds;' and in like manner, the Black Mountain tribes would implore assistance in vain from the 'Afreedees.' The 'Umbelah' expedition at one end of the Pathân frontier line, and the 'Muhsood' campaign at the other, may be accepted as giving a fairly accurate idea of the strength which the frontier clans could, under favourable circumstances, concentrate on a given point. At 'Umbelah' everything was in favour of a large hostile gathering of the tribes—our troops remained stationary and in a state of siege for nearly two months; the locality was within easy reach of the most powerful clans on the frontier, and religious pressure had been brought to bear by the local high priest; and yet, out of a fighting strength of probably 60,000, at no time were there more than 20,000 in arms against us. In the other expedition, the British force was isolated in the 'Muhsood' mountains for a fortnight, the tribe having had at least a month's previous warning of the approaching visitation. The Wuzeeree clans number at least 25,000, and, if the neighbouring Pathân tribes be taken into account, the total would probably exceed 40,000; and yet the numbers arrayed against us never perhaps reached 7000. This want of unity among Pathân races has been alluded to, pages 40, 43, 44, and whether the views recorded there be correct or not, the fact is evident that, with the utmost effort, and under the most favourable conditions, the border tribes generally cannot succeed in mustering more than a fifth or sixth of their fighting strength, even to repel an attack, still less to carry out an offensive movement.

CHAPTER IX.

*Systems of frontier management—In Scinde—In the Punjaub—
Duties of the Lieutenant-Governor in connection with it—
Pressure of work—Proposed change in system—Advantages
thereof—Policy of conciliation so called—Not successful—
Failure of Sir Lewis Pelly's mission—Detail of staff for
Border Commissioner.*

HAVING endeavoured to sketch briefly the characteristics and most important particulars connected with the Pathân tribes, we now proceed to consider the system under which frontier affairs have been carried on since our first appearance on the Affghan border in the spring of 1849.

It may be desirable to notice first (to dispose of the question so far as the present object is concerned) the comparative merits of the Scinde and Punjaub frontier administrations. The word 'comparative' has been used, but, in fact, no comparison can be instituted, for the conditions of the two localities differ so entirely, that there is no mutual ground on which to form an estimate of the respective merits of the two systems.

Thus, the Scinde frontier is mostly in the plains, and there are no inaccessible fastnesses for marauders to retreat to, like the 'Peerghul,' the 'Ghubur,' the

'Afreedee' mountains, the 'Mahâbun,' and the 'Black Mountain,' on the upper frontier. Consequently the force used in Scinde for the protection of the border consists mainly of cavalry, and their posts are located at a distance of fifty miles or more from the hills, approaching them only at the two extremities. This description is taken from a report by Major Jacob in 1854, but the line of protection is probably the same at the present time.

It is obvious that, having to deal with robbers and raiders in a comparatively open country, and with the dread that all hillmen have of cavalry, the work of retaliation and punishment must be much easier in Scinde than it is in a cramped and difficult country like that in the vicinity of the Affghan hills, in many parts of which it is impossible for cavalry to act, and where many of our villages are within a stone's throw of our hostile hill neighbours. As regards the military system of frontier management, then, that subsisting in Scinde need not further be noticed, except to remark that, under General Jacob's auspices, it has been a decided success. As regards the political administration, much stress has been laid by Scinde officers on the practice of treating the Bilooch border tribes as subjects of the Khan of Khelât, and they infer that the Punjaub Government should have adopted the same principle in regard to the Pathân tribes and the Ameer of Câbul. But it does not appear that this presumed responsibility of the Khan of Khelât has had much effect in dealing with the Bilooches, for, judging from an article in the 'Times' of November 1877, written by a strong advocate for the Scinde system, and presumably by one of General Jacob's old officers, it seems that the Khan of Khelât's authority over the tribes 'was only nominal, and was denied altogether by the more powerful tribes;' so that the influence exercised by him must have been altogether imaginary. In support of this view, the following remarks by Sir H. Green, Political Agent in Scinde, in the Biloochistan Blue-book, p. 516, are quoted:—

'The 'Murrees' being Bilooch, are certainly nominally subjects of the Khan of Khelât, and are held by him under the same control as the Afreedees of the hills surrounding the Peshawur valley are by the ruler of Câbul, and any complaint to the Khan would be of as much use as the Commissioner of Peshawur bringing to the notice of the Ameer of Câbul the conduct of the said 'Afreedees.'' This disposes conclusively of the advantages supposed to be derivable from considering the Bilooches as subjects of the Khan of 'Khelât,' and if this be so as regards the Khan of Khelât and the Bilooches, the relations between the great majority of the Pathân tribes and the Ameer of Câbul are of a still more vague and indefinite character.

The authority of the latter over the Pathâns is not even nominal, for he has never asserted it, except in the case of the 'Momunds,' and perhaps the 'Dourees;' so what possible 'beneficial results' would have been effected by setting up the Ameer as a 'dummy,' and telling the tribes when they had offended us that this was the person through whom they must account for their malpractices, it is difficult to conceive.

The writer in the 'Times' above quoted gives also some account of the Affghan frontier tribes, and impugns with some acrimony the Punjaub policy; but he is incorrect in some important details, and evidently has not the same personal acquaintance with his subject which he possesses in regard to Scinde; so the party accused may plead of this witness, *Nihil novit in causâ*.

The Scinde and Punjaub frontier lines meet at 'Kusmore,' at the southern extremity of the Derah Ghazi Khan district; and it is unfortunate, in the interests both of the Government and of the Bilooch border tribes, that there has been a constant irritation between the officials representing the Scinde and Punjaub administrations. This commenced at a very early date, almost immediately, indeed, after the annexation of the Punjaub. General (then Major) Jacob considered himself aggrieved by certain remarks contained in the first Punjaub Administration Report, in which it was stated that the Punjaub frontier force had to protect a more extended and more exposed line of frontier, on less pay and with fewer numbers, than the Scinde force possessed for guarding a limited and comparatively quiet border line.

In reply to this, Major Jacob endeavoured to show that the expenditure in Scinde was relatively less than that in the Punjaub, that the success had been greater, that the border tribes had been in great measure reclaimed, and that 'proximity to the hills was a very great advantage' to the protecting force. The words in inverted commas are Major Jacob's own, but his policy appears to have been at war with his opinions, for he had his posts removed to a distance of fifty miles notwithstanding.

The appointment of a Punjaub officer, Major Sandeman, to the Political Agency at 'Khelât,' will not, it is feared, tend to smooth matters over between the rival administrations. The move to Quettah and Khelât was General Jacob's own proposal in 1856, when it was negatived; it was brought forward again in 1865 by Sir Bartle Frere, but again rejected by the 'masterly inactive' politicians; and now that the measure has been finally carried out, instead of intrusting it to the Scinde Administration, whose offspring it was, the Punjaub tiger has stepped in and carried off the prey. This conflict of opinion and interests, combined with many other difficulties, appears to call for a united system of frontier government under one responsible head, and in considering the general question of border management, the agencies under which it is to be conducted are the first and most important.

At present, in the conduct of Punjaub border affairs, there are, first, the Deputy Commissioners of the frontier districts. These, as a rule, are the first to be brought in contact with the 'jirgahs,' and to them, in the first instance, are brought the reports of what is going on among the tribes. It is the duty of the Deputy Commissioners to keep the Commissioners thoroughly 'posted up' in all border affairs, and they are not allowed to take the initiative in any urgent matter without the sanction and approval of the Commissioners.

There are two Commissioners of Division on the frontier; the headquarters of one are at Peshawur, to whom are subordinate the districts of Peshawur, Huzârah, and Kohat; the other Commissioner is located at Derah Ismail Khan, and under him are the districts of Derah Ismail Khan, Bunnoo, and Derah Ghazi Khan. When the Commissioner is on the spot, as at Peshawur, he would take the principal portion of the frontier work himself, and the ordinary correspondence with Câbul is carried on by him without the Deputy Commissioner intervening. The Commissioner reports regularly, and specially when there is occasion, to the Secretary to the Punjaub Government, who lays the papers before the Lieutenant-Governor for his opinion and orders. The business then proceeds another stage to the Foreign Secretary to the Supreme Government, who, with a *précis*, brings the correspondence before the Viceroy for final orders, except when it has to go one step further to the Secretary of State for India. Thus the business passes through five or six channels before it reaches the final court for decision.

It seems hardly necessary to observe that the delay of this course of procedure must militate powerfully against promptness of decision, and that a question which has been passed through so many different offices must have gathered a vast amount of unnecessary and encumbering matter in the process.

The argument on the other side is, that there is advantage in the multitude of counsellors, and the subject receives fuller and more exhaustive treatment under the present system than it would experience if there were only one responsible head. More voluminous the treatment doubtless is, but whether more practical is fairly open to question. It appears impossible for the Governor of the Punjaub to give the undivided attention which is so urgently required for frontier affairs. Let any one take up one of the Annual Administration Reports of the Punjaub, and observe the multifarious topics which call on his time and energies, apart from border affairs. Upon the Lieutenant-Governor devolves the supervision of a country holding seventeen millions of inhabitants, the political superintendence of some fifteen or twenty quasi-independent native states within the Punjaub limits, and the conduct of political affairs with Cashmere beyond them. His civil administration includes, on the revenue side, the land revenue, surveys and settlements, Government and ward's estates, agriculture, trade, customs, mines, canals, forests, public works, and the working of telegraph and post-offices. On the judicial side, there are the civil and criminal law courts, all of which report regularly to the Governor annually, and make frequent special reports besides; the police and jail administrations, also regularly reported on; the great subject of sanitation, statistics, management of hospitals, the numberless and pressing claims of education throughout the province, and, finally, the correspondence connected with the Punjaub frontier force, numbering 12,000 men, which, as noted above, is still under the Civil Government.

Is it possible for one man, assisted as he is by a very limited staff, to do justice to all these subjects, and be able at the same time to devote the necessary care and attention to border jurisdiction—a subject which, weighty always, has become just now one of the gravest importance? The answer must be in the negative.

The Punjaub Government of course clings to the present system as part of a vested interest, but to all impartial observers it must be obvious that the pressure of other work is too great to allow of frontier affairs being thoroughly and carefully dealt with under existing circumstances. With reference to the subordinate frontier officers, the Punjaub Government itself has been obliged to admit, that 'Our danger now is not so much from the hostile disposition of the tribes, as from the fact that, owing to constant demands for reports of various kinds, the large increase of judicial business, and the increased care required in judicial procedure, our frontier officers are crushed with office-work, and have but little time for friendly personal communication with the border chiefs' (Punjaub Report, 1869–70).

The greater exceeds the less, and if the subordinates have little time for attending to special frontier work, *à fortiori* the Governor of the province cannot be expected to have any leisure to devote to this most important branch of his administration.

All this points to a measure which has been advocated for many years past—the appointment of a special Commissioner for the border provinces, who should be entirely independent of the Punjaub Government, and report direct to the Viceroy.

The internal administration of the Punjaub would not be the least affected by such a measure. The 'Indus' is a marked boundary of races, those on the east of the river being comparatively industrious and law-abiding peoples, among whom our regular system of government and administration of codified laws find favour and ready obedience; while on the west of the Indus we are brought almost immediately in contact with races who know not what law and a regular system of government mean, and who would be prepared to resist to the uttermost any attempts to have them enforced.

The administration of the Cis- and Trans-Indus districts is even now marked by considerable differences of treatment, it having been found necessary to pass special Acts with reference to the latter; and the sooner the whole frontier jurisdiction is placed on a new footing, the better for ourselves, and for our relations with the frontier tribes and with Câbul.

It will be necessary, however, to exercise a careful discrimination in the selection of the officer to hold the important post of frontier administrator. Special qualifications, such as firmness, energy, powers of conciliation, a strong will, and a knowledge of the character of the wild and fierce races he has to deal with, are what should be looked for in the pro-consul of the border provinces, who should enjoy also an entire freedom from other administrative harassments.

Personal government, above all other considerations, is what is mainly required in dealing with these wild races. They cannot understand the delays of office, or why it should be necessary to refer a simple matter to and fro half-a-dozen times before action is taken on it. These delays, and the hesitancy which has been shown to deal readily and decidedly with border questions, have to answer for most of our troubles on the Punjaub frontier. Instead of dealing promptly and at once with the affronts which we are constantly receiving from the hill tribes, the disposition has always been apparently to see how much the cup will hold before it overflows, and then we are obliged to undertake a troublesome and costly expedition to attain the same object, which might have been secured at half the expense and trouble if the blow had been struck at once.

If any of my readers should have access to the Punjaub Annual Administration Reports, I would ask them to look over the portion which treats of the political management of the border. There they will find, year after year, the statements of murder, robbery, and acts of violence committed by the hillmen on British subjects, and of the *guarantees* which have been taken from the tribes to prevent a repetition of these offences. These *guarantees* are sometimes the suspension of the payment for the Kohât Pass, sometimes the promises of the tribe for future good behaviour (!), sometimes the taking of hostages. The last would be the only substantial guarantee of the lot, but I believe that it is never thoroughly carried into effect. The hostages are kept at Peshawur probably for a while, until the tribe has been 'good' for a month or two, and then they are released to work fresh mischief. If they were sent off to Lahore or Delhi, and kept there for a year or more, and were then relieved by a fresh batch of hostages, the measure might have some effect, but the

THE 'CONCILIATION' POLICY.

only argument the hillmen really understand is that *ad baculum*.

Much has been said and written of the policy of conciliation towards the frontier tribes. Sir Charles Wood, in his despatch to the Governor-General after the Umbelah campaign, thus discusses the subject. After stating that 'an aggressive policy is wholly opposed to the wishes of Her Majesty's Government, as being contrary to the true interests of the state,'—as if it had been our practice to anticipate attacks and make aggressions, instead of waiting and waiting till very shame compelled us to assert our power,—he says, 'Our true course ought to be, not to interfere in their internal concerns, but to cultivate friendly relations with them, and to endeavour to convince them, by our forbearance and kindly conduct, that their wisest plan is to be on good terms with us, in order that they may derive those advantages from intercourse with us which are sure to follow from the interchange of commodities and mutual benefits.' This sounds plausible enough, but Sir Charles Wood evidently was not fully cognisant of the antecedents, and that forbearance and kindly conduct on our part had been already carried to their extremest limits. We endured the violence, robbery, and constant attacks of the Muhsood Wuzeerees for ten years before we retaliated in 1860. The Umbelah expedition in 1863 was the consequence of the forbearance exercised towards the hill tribes and Hindostânees in the expedition against them in 1858 under Sir Sydney Cotton. The insults we have received from the Afreedees are without number and without cessation, and the expedition now undertaken against them (November 1877) was only resolved on after a long series of affronts and injuries, which have formed the subject of a special minute by the Viceroy.

If we have succeeded in giving anything like an accurate representation of the character of the hill tribes, it will be evident to the reader that these savage people cannot appreciate a kindly and conciliatory course of treatment, until they have been made thoroughly to realise that the power which forbears can also punish. Their view is that, from apprehension of *them*, attempts at conciliation on our part mean simply, 'Please don't do it again.' They see that we suffer our villages to be harried, our subjects robbed and murdered, and yet we make no sign; and while we are thinking they are acting. We have not yet—

'Learned that fearful commenting
Is leaden servitor to dull delay.'

Nor, to finish the quotation, that—

'Our counsel should be our shield.
We should be brief when *robbers* take the field.'

There would be good hope if we had a man upon the spot with a thorough knowledge of the situation, treating directly with the representatives of the tribes, receiving them himself, and letting them feel that he had the power to punish as well as the will to conciliate, the gauntlet of steel in the glove of velvet; in fact, making them realise the power of personal government, and that the usual formulæ of subterfuges, promises to be good in future, and immaterial guarantees, availed no longer.

Of course, as has been said above, special qualities are required for such a representative of British authority on the frontier, but the men are to be found if preferment is allowed to go by desert, and not by letter and affection. Durand, Edwardes, James, Nicholson, Taylor are among the names of the past who would have done ample justice to the position. In the present, there are the two Lumsdens, Watson, &c., and doubtless other rising men to be found; but to send a representative who has no other qualification than that of talent or of success in a totally different sphere of action, would be to court failure.

A mistake of this kind was made, as many think, in sending Sir Lewis Pelly to Peshawur in the summer of 1877 to negotiate with the Ameer of Câbul's representative. There is nothing to be said against Sir Lewis Pelly, who is a highly esteemed servant of the Government; but he brought the worst of all recommendations for his ambassadorial work in his ignorance of the people, the country, and the situation. Further, he was placed in a false position as regarded the person through whom the Câbul correspondence is mainly carried on, viz., the Commissioner of Peshawur. The latter officer appears to have been completely set aside in the communications between Sir Lewis Pelly and the Câbul envoy, which was not only an unnecessary slight to the Commissioner, but must have militated very strongly against any chance Sir Lewis Pelly might have had of bringing the negotiations to a successful issue, by depriving him of the advantage of the local and political experience of the Commissioner. This would be necessarily great from his work and position, and it was enhanced in the present instance from the fact of the officer now holding the post, Sir R. Pollock, having been at Peshawur for the last ten years.

Under these circumstances, only a failure of Sir Lewis Pelly's mission could have been anticipated, and the result justified the expectation.

Besides the officer intrusted with the management of the frontier and Câbul affairs, there would be the usual staff of officers for the transaction of civil business, and doubtless a few to act as political assistants or secretaries to the Chief Commissioner; but the civil work of the frontier should be minimised, by which is meant that the dreary system of long reports and elaborate statistics, which form such a burthen to the majority of Punjaub civil officers, should be reduced to its smallest limit. The civil staff might remain much as it is at present, the Civil Commissioner being endowed with larger powers. At present the Commissioner sentences to death in extreme cases, but the order is subject to the approval of the chief court. The final issue might be left now with the frontier Commissioners, or the Chief Commissioner might take the place of the chief court as regards death sentences, but he certainly should not be encumbered with hearing and passing orders in appeal cases.

These matters of detail might be arranged without much difficulty; and if, as some people think, there is too much law already in the Punjaub, it is most desirable that all superfluity of the article should be eliminated from the frontier districts.

CHAPTER X.

Method of dealing with the frontier tribes—Policy of prompt chastisement not properly carried out—Causes of the same—Character of various expeditions against the tribes—That against the Jowâkees—Means available for carrying out expeditions.

WE come now to consider the mode of dealing with Câbul and the frontier tribes. Taking the latter first, the argument may fairly be commenced with the assumption that the course hitherto pursued has been a failure. Sir Charles Wood, in his despatch already quoted, while inculcating the necessity of conciliatory treatment, and deprecating distant and costly expeditions, is obliged to admit that there are circumstances under which 'individuals or tribes who injure our subjects or make inroads on our districts must be summarily and severely punished' (par. 17); and 'there are no doubt cases in which it may be requisite that lightly equipped and well-selected detachments should penetrate for short distances into the hills, and destroy the towers, rendezvous, and places of assembly of the offending tribes' (par. 21); and the Punjaub Government has uniformly insisted on the necessity of promptness of action in chastising offending tribes. How is it, then, that this policy has not been consistently carried out? The answer is not difficult to find. The Punjaub Government fears what the Viceroy may say. The Viceroy doubts before the Secretary of State—and the Secretary of State hesitates in presence of public opinion. All deference is due undoubtedly to an intelligent and well-educated public opinion, but unfortunately, in regard to India, the public opinion in England is neither intelligent nor well informed. We shall probably be well within the mark if we assume that there is not more than one in five hundred of educated Englishmen who has the remotest conception of what the North-West frontier is, of what nationality the tribes which inhabit it are composed, or of the policy pursued towards them; and if England will not educate itself so far as to acquire some little knowledge of its most important possession, then the public opinion in England should not be taken into account.

An attempt has been made in the preceding pages to describe the varying character of expeditions against the hill tribes—the short, sharp, and decisive, as in Nicholson's descent on the 'Oomurzye' in 1853; the more protracted visitations, as in the 'Muhsood' expedition of 1860; and the greatly extended scale of operations, as exemplified in the 'Umbelah' campaign of 1863. It can hardly be said, perhaps, that complete success has attended any of these military demonstrations. The 'Muhsoods,' it is true, have never again attempted a movement in strength beyond the shelter of their hills, as in 1860, but they have been constantly troublesome since as pilferers and robbers. The scheme of the Umbelah campaign was intended to include the punishment of the 'Hussunzye' and other Black Mountain tribes, but that portion of the programme was omitted in consequence of the unexpected opposition we met with at 'Umbelah,' and failing the lesson which should have been inflicted then, it became necessary to send a force against the Black Mountain tribes in 1868, which failed in effecting anything decisive, as noted above.

Nicholson's raid upon the 'Oomurzye' was perhaps the most successful in its results of the three expeditions named, and it is to operations of that character, I think, that we should look, in all but extreme cases, for the preservation of peace on the border. Another instance may be given of a rapid and effectual attack upon a village near 'Peshawur' in August 1877, extracted from the 'Times of India.' Certain Afreedees about the 'Kohât' Pass had failed (as usual) to carry out the stipulations which they had entered into during the month of March previous to keep open the pass. A week was given them to consider, at the end of which time they sent an impertinent reply to our just demands. On the night of the 14th August, a small body of troops, consisting of two guns H.A., a troop of Bengal cavalry, and sixty rifles of the 14th Sikh regiment, the infantry riding in 'ekkas' (the one-horse chaise of the country), started for the recusant village, which they reached before daybreak and quietly surrounded. When the villagers turned out at daybreak for their usual avocations, and found what a predicament they were in, they surrendered at discretion, gave up their arms, and tendered several heads of families as hostages. The troops returned to quarters within the twenty-four hours. So far as it went, this result was highly satisfactory, but it is to be feared that the usual extreme 'forbearance' may have been observed in this case also, and the arms and hostages returned after a brief detention. It would seem as if something of the kind had occurred, for at the present writing (December 1877), a petty tribe, the Jowakees, also connected with the 'Kohât' Pass, are in open conflict with the Government.

It is satisfactory to observe that the Government appears determined to visit this last affront with signal punishment. The force under General Keyes has already been some time in the 'Jowakee' country, and has destroyed several strongholds; and its continual presence in their hills, contrary to the usual practice of punishing and departing at once, is likely to make the refractory 'Jowakees' feel keenly the retribution they have invited. We have ample means for carrying out these sudden invasions ready at hand in the Punjaub frontier force. Mule-carriage, the readiest means for the movement of troops in the hills, is always kept up by the frontier regiments; the men are used to hill warfare; the mountain batteries can go anywhere; and the commissariat for a week's supply for the troops is always at hand. If these splendid resources had been always and readily applied to the purpose for which they were specially organised, viz., the prompt punishment of injuries and affronts received from the border tribes, we might have been in a better position now, but, as we have attempted to show above, the fear of departing from the policy of conciliation at all costs, which has been so unreasonably insisted on, has cramped the energies of our border officials, and thus 'I dare not waits upon I would' to the end of the chapter. We believe that, as a general rule, small expeditions of the nature described above, with the results when attained carried to their legitimate issue, would change the aspect of affairs on the frontier. The captured arms should be destroyed and not restored, the hostages be made to feel some of the real inconveniences which should attach to their position, and the tribes by these and similar means made to understand that we were in earnest in our resolution to maintain the peace of our border, and no long time would elapse before that end was attained.

It is hardly necessary to observe that these expeditions should not be organised until conciliation in its proper sense had been fairly tried. The Chief Commissioner would point out to the offending tribe the advisability of a ready and complete reparation for the injury done, would fix the time within which satisfaction was to be rendered, and would let them understand at the same time that if they failed to comply there would be no more *pourparlers*, but swift and ample retribution. One or two lessons of this kind would probably bring about a good understanding between ourselves and the frontier tribes, those, at least, within easy reach of us. It is, of course, possible that we may be brought face to face with complications of greater magnitude than border raids, but in all such cases it would be a great help to us to know that we had made our border neighbours feel from personal experience our power to deal with them at least, and this would probably prevent them from joining any combinations against us.

The prompt expedition, then, such as that of Nicholson against the Oomurzye, that against certain of the Pass 'Afreedees,' quoted at p. 122, and that by Keyes against the 'Buzôtees,' having proved the most successful, should form the patterns of future military undertakings.

For pacific means, the two principal ones are inducing men of the frontier to enlist in our regiments, and offering land within our border to the hill tribes for purposes of colonisation. This latter has answered wonderfully with the 'Hâtee Khail' Wuzeerees, who, as above noted, were worked upon by the fear of losing their fields and cultivation to perform the almost unprecedented act of giving up a fellow-tribesman for capital punishment. It has had a good effect also with the 'Oomurzye,' and doubtless with many others. The attempt has been made, as before recorded, to induce the 'Muhsoods' to colonise, but hitherto it does not appear to have been attended with much success; and that tribe would perhaps be the last to welcome civilisation in any form, from their comparatively isolated position and the wild habits which that isolation involves. But example will do much, and when they see men of the branches of their own tribe reaping the advantages of civilised life, it is to be hoped that time will bring them round to follow their lead.

Regarding the first means of pacification advocated, that of enlisting men of the border tribes into our regiments, a writer in one of the papers has deprecated the practice on account of the faithlessness of the Pathâns to their salt, and stated that instances of desertion from their regiments by these men, carrying their arms with them, were very common. Times must indeed have changed in the brief interval which has elapsed since the author knew the Punjaub frontier force if this assertion be correct, but he is convinced that the writer is altogether misinformed. On looking through his letter for some proof of his statements, the only tangible evidence that could be found was, that in one of the skirmishes lately in the neighbourhood of the 'Kohât' Pass, a Government rifle was taken from an Afreedee, said to have been a sepoy of the 29th Punjaub infantry (*not* one of the frontier regiments). All the rest was mere assertion and hearsay, which, it was satisfactory to see, was stoutly contradicted by a subsequent writer. All our experience for the last twenty years goes to disprove this calumny on the Pathân soldiers.

The position at 'Umbelah' might be taken as a crucial test. The men were fighting then against their own relatives and against their own spiritual pastor, the 'Akhûnd.' They were exposed for two months to the incessant reproaches of the 'Bonair' and other Pathân tribes, which were launched against them in the midst of the fighting and whenever opportunity offered; and among the large number of Pathân soldiers with the

'Umbelah' force, the solitary instance of desertion was that of a young 'Bonair' recruit, who had only lately joined his regiment. This speaks volumes; and we may repeat, therefore, that by inducing men of the border tribes to enlist, we should greatly assist the process of pacification.

We do not know if it has ever occurred to the authorities to try and purchase the tongue of 'Afreedee' land which intervenes between Peshawur and the Kohât districts, and at the head of which is the cause of all our troubles, the Kohât Pass. We might most justly have annexed it after all the hostility which its inhabitants have evinced towards us, and the many affronts and injuries we have sustained at their hands, but it would, of course, be better if our object could be obtained by purchase or exchange. Undoubtedly there would be considerable difficulties in the way—the difficulty of inducing an Affghan to give up his land and birthright; the probability that, for some time, at least, we should have to provide carefully against violence and rapine, and so forth; but eventually, and that possibly after no long interval, matters would settle down, and we should be rid of one of the chief elements which make the management of the 'Kohât' Pass so complicated a political problem.

CHAPTER XI.

Political dealings with Câbul—Hostility of the Affghans during the 'Sikh' war of 1848-49—Change of feeling—Application of Ameer Dost Mohamed to the Governor-General—Subsidies of money and arms granted—Strife for the succession after Dost Mohamed's death—Final success of Sher Ali—His feelings towards us—His visit to Lord Mayo in 1869—Character of Sher Ali—The conciliation policy—Advantages of the move to Quettah—Lord Lawrence's opinion on the subject—Remarks thereon.

OUR dealings with 'Câbul' have gone through several phases. It was unfortunate that our first connection with that kingdom should have given a sense of injury to the 'Affghans,' the remains whereof rankle perhaps to the present day; and that we should have received such wrongs at their hands as made the ears of all Englishmen who heard of them to tingle. It was a bad preparation for the cordiality of our relations in the future. It is beside the present question to discuss the merits of our intervention in 'Câbul' in 1838-41. Generally, it could have been neither just nor politic to attempt to thrust upon the 'Câbulees' a king whom the nation detested. It is not likely that we should ever again undertake so useless and so losing a venture, but the unhappy failure of our agents in those transactions may, or should, give us a lesson in making selection of our political chiefs for the future. Divided counsels and delay in seizing opportunities were the causes of all our disasters in 'Câbul,' and it is to be hoped that similar mistakes in future may not reproduce the same misfortunes.

Our relations with 'Câbul' appear to have been of a distant character for some years after our withdrawal from that country in 1842, but the continued hostility of the Affghans was evinced by their sending a cavalry contingent to assist the Sikh rebel leaders in 1848-49. This contingent took a part in the battle of Goojerât, before described, but fled incontinently on being charged by our cavalry. After this there appears to have been little intercourse between the Governments until the autumn of 1854, when the Ameer Dost Mahomed sent a friendly letter to the Governor-General. This was favourably considered, and in the following year an offensive and defensive alliance was contracted between the 'Câbul' state and the British Government. In the following year Dost Mahomed applied to the Governor-General for assistance against the Persians, who were besieging Herât. This was acknowledged by the despatch of 4000 muskets and a sum of £50,000, but this subsidy arrived too late to save Herât, which was taken by the Persians in 1856. In January 1857 Dost Mahomed had an interview with Sir J. Lawrence, then Chief Commissioner of the Punjaub, at Peshawur, the result of which was that a further subsidy of £10,000 per mensem was granted him to assist in the payment of his troops and to provide for the defence of his country. At the same time a mission of British officers, consisting of the two Lumsdens and Dr. Bellew, was despatched to assist and advise the Ameer.

One of the consequences of our successes in the war with Persia in 1856–57 was the restoration of Herât to Câbul, and in gratitude for this the Ameer exerted himself to prevent any of his subjects from taking part against us during the Mutiny.

Our relations with 'Câbul' continued to be of a friendly order until the death of Dost Mahomed in June 1863. After his death there arose a war for the succession to the throne. 'Sher Ali' had been nominated as the 'Wulee-ahud,' or heir-apparent, by Dost Mahomed, but the elder brothers, Mahomed Ufzul and Mahomed Azim, asserted their claims, and civil war commenced, which lasted with varying results till 1868. For the first two years Sher Ali had the best of it, and was recognised by the British Government as king *de facto*, but they declined to hail him as such *de jure*. This created no small amount of hostile feeling in his bosom towards us, which was doubtless enhanced by the Governor-General successively recognising Mahomed Ufzul, when he got the ascendant in 1867–68, and, on his death, for a brief period, Mahomed Azim also, as *de facto* sovereigns of Câbul. 'Sher Ali' was successful at last in quelling all opposition, and succeeded formally to the throne of Câbul in August 1868.

The above circumstances should be borne in mind

in considering 'Sher Ali's' conduct towards us. With him the remembrance of slight injuries is graven on the rock, and the record of weighty favours received written in the sand. Treacherous, fickle, and ungrateful, an Affghan of the Affghans is he.

In the autumn of 1868, Sher Ali proposed to meet the Governor-General, Sir John Lawrence, at Peshawur, but was unable to carry out his intention in consequence of the hostile front shown by his nephew, Abdurahman Khan, who was still in arms against the Ameer's government. Sir John Lawrence, however, sent the Ameer £60,000 and 6000 stand of arms; and in the following spring Sher Ali came to meet Lord Mayo at Umballah. He was most royally entertained, and sent home full of presents and promises. As a consequence of his approval of what he had seen among us, he ordered a 'Pukhtoo' translation to be made of the manual and platoon exercises, and an edict was issued prohibiting cobblers from making shoes of any other than the European pattern!

Relations continued friendly for some years, during which interval the Ameer begged the British Government to arrange the boundaries between Câbul and Persia in Seistân, which was undertaken by Sir F. Goldsmid and other officers on the part of the British Government.

In 1872 there arose differences between the Ameer and his son Yâkoob Khan, which have been rankling more or less ever since; and within the last year or so, Sher Ali has begun to show an unfriendly, if not a hostile, aspect to the British. It will be seen that for the last twenty years, at least, our conduct towards the State of Câbul has been not only friendly, but liberal in the highest degree. We had little to expect from the Ameer in return for our good offices, and the very substantial proof of our amity which we have given him in the shape of arms and money. He could not help us in keeping our border quiet, because he had neither influence nor authority over our turbulent frontier neighbours. 'Câbul' is not a country which is of much use to us in a commercial point of view, and our subjects cannot trade with it in consequence of the dangers of the road.

The only thing required of Sher Ali, and which, after our uniform liberality, we had a right to expect from him, was that he should hold to our friendship, and not allow himself to be drawn by Russia into an alliance detrimental to our interests; and this latter course, with the customary faithlessness of the Affghan race, and with the obstinacy which is peculiar to his own nature, he appears to be bent on pursuing. Kindness and conciliation are of little use in dealing with Sher Ali, as events have pretty clearly demonstrated; and if we are not prepared to make him agree to our proposal of having a Resident at Câbul with a high hand, we had better leave him alone altogether. Sweet words and subsidies are alike thrown away on a character like this, and the latter probably would be used to our detriment at the first opportunity. Under this view, we consider the move to Quettah and Khelât to have been a most desirable one, as showing this barbarian ruler that we are determined at last to assert our position. The most inactive of the 'masterly inactive' party cannot deny that we have exhausted conciliation in our dealings with 'Câbul,' and unless we are prepared to carry out the 'inactive' policy to the uttermost, and allow the uncivilised ruler of a neighbour state to laugh us to scorn, and to receive our rival with open arms, the sooner we assert ourselves the better. The course of events has conferred an importance on Câbul and its ruler which we cannot afford to overlook or underrate.

So long as there existed no question of Russian intrigue, or of a probability of the Ameer being cajoled into an alliance with that state, we could afford to allow 'Sher Ali' to sulk as he pleased; but now that Russia has commenced her usual game of flattering and cajoling the Ameer, as a preparatory step to swallowing him, and as the latter is evincing a dangerous disposition to dally with his tempter, it is time for us to show that we are in earnest. The conceit of Sher Ali is great. He regards himself as 'Aflatoon-i-zumanâh,' as the Persians say—the Plato of the age—and flatters himself, doubtless, that he shall be able to outwit the Russians, and fleece them as he has fleeced us, not knowing the character of the nation he has to deal with, and ignorant that she has in the school of deceit taken a far higher degree than the clumsy best of an uncivilised Affghan. With reference to the importance which Affghanistan from its position has lately assumed, the following is quoted from Wallace's 'Russia:'—'Russia must push forward her frontier until she reaches a country possessing a government which is willing and able to keep order within its boundaries, and to prevent its subjects from committing depredations on their neighbours. As none of the petty states of Central Asia seem capable of permanently fulfilling this condition, it is pretty certain that the Russian and British frontiers will one day meet. Where they will meet depends on ourselves. If we do not wish our rival to overstep a certain line, we must advance to that line. As to the complications and disputes which inevitably arise between contiguous nations, I think they are fewer and less dangerous than those which arise between nations separated from each other by a small state, which is incapable of making its neutrality respected, and is kept alive simply by the mutual jealousy of rival powers . . . . The old story that great powers may be made to keep the peace by interposing small independent states between them is long since exploded' (vol. ii. p. 440). The general purport of this all will agree with, and the appearance of the first Cossack on the left bank of the Oxus should be the signal for the movement of British troops from Peshawur on Câbul and from Quettah on Candahar and Herât.

Judging from Sir Lewis Pelly's failure to induce the Ameer to receive a British Resident at his court, and from the reports which abound in the Indian papers that Sher Ali is taking measures to increase his army, it would seem that we must be on the point of rupture with that ruler, if indeed it has not already taken place. It is only to be hoped that our action will be firm and determined. It cannot be too often repeated that no trust whatever is to be placed in the professions or in the most solemn promises of the 'Câbul' despot. This has been proved over and over again, and yet our policy seems to travel in the old groove—

> 'Trusting again, to be again undone.'

Lord Lawrence has lately written a long letter to the 'Times' on this subject, and as he is justly supposed to speak with authority, it may be as well to examine some of his arguments. His objections to the occupation of Quettah appear to be based on three considerations. First, the expense which is likely to attend the measure; secondly, that it would be better to await the attack of an enemy on our own base (the eastern) of the Affghan mountains than to advance our posts; and thirdly, that the Affghans would take umbrage at the measure. To the first objection it may be answered, that large interests and vast countries cannot be protected without cost, and, on the other side, that a judicious outlay now may save us sums untold in the future. We hope it is not ungenerous to add, that if the movement to Quettah had been effected when it was first proposed by General Jacob in 1856, or even when it was renewed by Sir Bartle Frere in 1865, both the expense and the difficulties attending the measure would have been far less than they are likely to be now. It was Sir John Lawrence, it is believed, who negatived Sir Bartle Frere's proposal, and he is only consistent in deprecating the movement now. But the argument by which Lord Lawrence supports his view, viz., that it would be better to meet a hostile army at the eastern foot of the Affghan hills, rather than encounter it farther on, is equivalent to saying that it is better to receive the attack of a besieging force in the citadel rather than meet it at the outworks. By allowing a hostile army to move through the rugged and difficult defiles of the Affghan mountains unopposed, and in suffering him to concentrate his battalions under their cover before making his descent upon the plains, we should lose all the strategical advantages we might derive from occupying strong posts on the hills for impeding and harassing his movements. We should be placed also at the moral disadvantage of receiving instead of delivering the attack; and even if successful at first, the pursuit of a defeated army into the mountains is a difficult and dangerous measure, especially as our enemy would have been careful to maintain, what we are recommended to neglect, fortified posts in the hills to cover his retreat and enable him to reform his columns.

The very fact, too, of our adopting such a timid policy would probably do more to raise disaffection among our subjects in India than the apparent remoteness of our army in the hills would encourage it, as Lord Lawrence appears to apprehend, especially as we should have the guarantee of the brothers, sons, and husbands of our subjects in India forming part of our advance force.

It must be recognised, however, that a great political difficulty exists in the probability of disaffection being stirred up among the natives by Russian agents, and there will be occasion to offer a few remarks on the subject presently.

With Quettah strongly occupied, a good road through

the Bolân Pass, and a branch railway from the Indus Valley line to the mouth of the pass, we should hold a strong strategical position or *point d'appui* from whence a movement to Candahar and Herât might be effected with comparative ease. The distance from Quettah to Candahar is about 150 miles, from Candahar to Câbul about 200, and from Candahar to Herât about 280; so that, in point of time, there would be very little delay in placing a strong force before any of the positions named. It would not appear to be necessary at present to do more than hold Quettah. We have an undeniable right to do this by treaty, and unpalatable as the project may be to the Affghans, it is so obviously safe and necessary a measure for us, in the prospect of future complications, that it should be carried out at all risks.

The occupation of Quettah should not be considered as a threat to Affghanistan, nor as necessarily indicating a purpose on our part of advancing still farther. The quarrels between the Khan of Khelât and the Bilooch chiefs had reached to such a height, and compromised so seriously the safety and well-being of our border, that when, at the invitation of both parties, we came in to arbitrate, and it may be to manage affairs for them, it was most desirable that the hands of the future Resident at Khelât should be strengthened by the location of a military force in the country, a contingency which had been foreseen and provided for in previous treaties. If it should so happen that the measure gives us advantages separate from and in addition to our interest in Khelât affairs, let us take them and be thankful, without further question. Of course the step is unpalatable to the Affghans. It breaks up the 'purdah,' as they term it, of their country, of which all the hill-tribes are so jealous, tears away the veil, and betrays the weak places. At Quettah we are inside and in rear of the 'Suleimânee' and other mountain ranges, which have always been looked on as such formidable obstacles; and holding Quettah at one end of the line and Peshawur at the other, we could sweep down on Câbul whenever it so pleased us. As regards the opposition we should be likely to meet with, and which is somewhat insisted on by Lord Lawrence, let the reader look back at the advance of Nott from Candahar, and of Pollock from Peshawur in 1842–43, and observe the ease with which those generals swept away all Affghan opposition, and then let him consider the incalculable improvement that has taken place in our weapons since that time, and reduce the question to a rule-of-three sum. If troops armed with the old 'Brown Bess,' and possessing only the artillery of that period, could drive the Affghans off the hills as they did in 1842–43, what will a force armed with the Henry-Martini rifle, supplied with field-guns of marvellous precision, and with light mountain pieces which can go anywhere, be able to effect in 1878?

We have supplied the Affghan chief of late years with a large number of arms, but we may trust that we have not yet quite gone the length of furnishing his arsenal with Snider rifles, that he may 'hoist us with our own petard.' The statement is made under correction, however. We may fairly, then, speak of the military difficulties attending a move on Candahar or

Herât as not worth considering. With reference to the point urged by Lord Lawrence, that in occupying Quettah and threatening Candahar we shall give umbrage to the Affghan ruler and his people, and 'do much to destroy all the good that has flowed from our conciliatory and kindly disposition towards them during the last twenty years,' it may not be unreasonable to ask what *is* the good which has resulted from this amiable treatment of the Ameer on our part? There may be matter in the archives of the Foreign Office to show good service rendered by the rulers of Cabul to us, but it is not patent to the public. The only service generally urged, and that of a negative kind, was that Dost Mahomed kept quiet during the Mutiny; but he was even then receiving subsidies of money and arms from our Government, and was hopeful of much more; moreover, he had quite enough on his own hands at the time, with internal troubles and possible complications with Persia, to admit of his making any decided movement against us. I think, under these circumstances, that our debt of gratitude to the 'Affghans' on this score is not a heavy one, especially as, on the other side of the account, the mission of British officers which was sent to Affghanistan at that time received very scurvy and unworthy treatment at the hands of the Affghans.

With the single exception above noted, if exception it can be called, the record of transactions between us since 1843 consists of a long list of substantial favours conferred on our part, while the opposite page of the account is a blank; and within the last few months the

Ameer's conduct in resisting our advances and tampering with Russia to our detriment shows pretty clearly that there is no intention on his part of requiting our past good offices in the only way practicable.

The conciliation policy has had its run for a quarter of a century, both with the rulers of Affghanistan and with the border tribes, and if its advocates can point to any satisfactory results which it has achieved, let them do so by all means. If, as ordinary observers of facts would opine, none such are forthcoming, surely it is time to try a change. If a course of policy can show no good fruits after twenty-five years of operation, it is a mere truism to say that it is a failure; and in the present very critical times we cannot afford to prolong failures for the sake of sentiment. Let us hope, then, that the Quettah movement will be firmly and determinedly carried out, without any further reference to the sentiments of the ruler or people of Affghanistan. We owe them nothing certainly; all their actions towards us have been obstructive, and will continue so to the end; and, as has been repeatedly stated, they cannot appreciate the purport of honourable and conciliatory treatment, though they are always ready to take advantage of it. The writer remembers an old Sikh chief, with whom he was discoursing during the Punjaub troubles in 1848–49, giving an illustration of our position then which might apply now. Speaking of the situation then, when Lahore only was under control, all the rest of the province being in the throes of rebellion, he compared it to a sheet with one large stone in the centre only, and the skirts flying up to all the winds of heaven. 'But,' said he, 'place stones at the four corners also, and you have your sheet under control.' Thus, with Quettah occupied in strength at one extremity of Affghanistan and Peshawur at the other, a strong central position at Agra or Delhi, and the seaports of Calcutta and Bombay well garrisoned, we should have our sheet secured in the centre and at the four corners.

CHAPTER XII.

General remarks on the feelings of the natives of India towards the English—The Mohammedans—Opinions regarding them — Sir R. Temple — Vambéry — Sir G. Campbell—'Fraser's Magazine'—Major Osborn — Other opinions on this subject—State of feeling among Hindoos and others—Effects in India of rapid changes.

It is proposed to offer, in conclusion, a few general remarks on the topic of our native fellow-subjects in India, the present state of our relations towards them, and the nature of their feelings towards us; and we commence with the Mohammedans, who, though far from being the most numerous, are the most influential, and the most difficult to deal with, of all our Indian subjects. In the discussions which have arisen on this subject, the general tendency of opinion appears to be that the feeling of the Mohammedans towards us constitutes a source of danger to our interests in India, and Kaye in his 'History of the Mutiny' gives no obscure intimations of his opinion that they were the mainspring of the revolt.

That the Mussulman races of India should regard us with dislike, independent of any special causes operating to promote disaffection among them, is not to be wondered at. With them—we speak of the educated and respectable (for the lower Mussulmans of India are little better than Hindoos in the matter of caste observances and knowledge of their creed),—with them there is the ever-present recollection of the antecedent glory and dominion of their religion, now existing on sufferance, and admitted to equal privileges only with the contemned creed of the idolatrous Hindoo; and the descendants of the former conquerors and rulers of the land must now be content to share the dole of *their* conquerors with the despised race whom they had trodden under foot. All this to the formerly dominant race, whose character is formed mainly on their creed, aggressive, intolerant and overweening, must be gall and wormwood, and their dissatisfaction with the present state of things, even if no exceptional circumstances were present, is not question of argument, but of fact. With all deference to the opinions which have been recorded on this subject—and some of them are well entitled to consideration and respect—it is to be feared that the Mohammedans of India as a body are disloyal and secretly hostile to us, and that in the event of another outbreak they would be found, as they were in the revolt of 1857, the main instigators of the movement, and the chief agents in the persecution and destruction of our people.

It is no reply to this to say, that some members of the Mohammedan faith behaved nobly during the Mutiny, and ranged themselves on our side when their co-religionists were wading in English blood.

The rareness of the instances, and the *empressement* with which they were brought forward by the advocates for Mohammedan loyalty, are sufficient proof of their exceptional character. Of course, there are men to be found even now who will uphold the Mohammedans to be loyal and faithful subjects of the Queen, just as in the Mutiny many excellent and experienced officers adhered to their belief in the incorruptible fidelity of the sepoy, and in too many instances sealed their fatal credulity with their life's blood.

It would not be difficult to support these views by quotations from the published opinions of men well qualified to judge. Sir Richard Temple, in one of the reports presented to Parliament under the title of 'Systems of Government,' has expressed himself very strongly as to the hostility entertained towards us by the Mohammedan priesthood, and Vambéry in his 'Sketches in Central Asia,' commenting on Muscovite intrigues, uses even stronger language with reference to the Indian Mohammedans. These remarks apply mainly, of course, to the religious side of the question, the character of the Moslem as formed on the Koran, and it is difficult to conceive how from that teaching a strict Mohammedan can be a loyal subject of an alien and (as they would term it) an infidel Government. As a late writer in the 'Quarterly' has phrased it, 'Rebellion is with them a religious duty as against a heathen Government.'

At the same time there is a social aspect to the question which presents more favourable features. The Mohammedans have of late years proved themselves good and faithful soldiers, even that wild and bigoted section of them which is recruited from the border tribes, as has been previously noticed; and the promptness which has been evinced by Mohammedans to volunteer for service in Europe now is not only a satisfactory indication of their readiness to serve us, but it furnishes a pretty conclusive answer to the arguments of those who have asserted that the Mohammedans of India have no interest in common with their co-religionists in Turkey.

It may be considered fortunate that our line of policy during the present complications has not taken the direction of 'coercing' the Turks, for in that case the religious element might have made itself dangerously prominent in India, and such a contingency should never be lost sight of or treated lightly in our conduct of affairs in India.

But let us hear also what those who hold the opposite views on this subject have to say for themselves.

Sir George Campbell, who held the office of Lieutenant-Governor of Bengal for some time, has proclaimed his opinion that there is little danger of Mohammedan disaffection in India; that of the forty millions of Mohammedans in that country, twenty millions are in Eastern Bengal, and they are the best and quietest of subjects; the ten millions of Mohammedans in the Punjaub are quiet and industrious, and make good subjects. All this is true *at present*. So long as there is no disturbing element at hand, so long as they are permitted to cultivate their fields and earn their bread in peace, why should they not be quiet; but does Sir George Campbell know so little of the native temper and of the clanship of the Mohammedan religion as to suppose that we could

K

reckon on the quietude and fidelity of our Mussulman subjects if anything affecting the interest or welfare of their creed were to present itself, any measure of conquest or annexation in contemplation, by which it might be supposed (and we all know how painfully susceptible and credulous natives of India are in matters affecting their religion) that the Moslem faith and its representatives were in danger? Whether Sir George Campbell has had any special opportunities of obtaining an insight into the feelings of the Mohammedans of Bengal we do not know, but with reference to the ten millions of Mussulmans in the Punjaub, we take leave to express a directly contrary opinion to that recorded by the late Governor of Bengal.

There is hardly an officer in the Punjaub who has held charge of a district in that province for any length of time who has not at one time or another experienced trouble and difficulty from the religious proclivities of the Mohammedans of his district. Now it is a movement against the missionaries' work in the villages; anon there is a mysterious document found in some village mosque, of whose origin there is no trace, purporting generally to be an exhortation from Mecca, warning the faithful to be vigilant, and containing cautions and prophecies of some portentous event shortly to be expected. These missives occur every now and then, like the mysterious 'chupattie' before the Mutiny. The author has had experience of two or three of them during his career as district officer. Then there are frequent religious squabbles between the Mussulmans and Hindoos, often assuming a troublesome if not a dangerous character. There is a constant source of trouble, too, in the fanatical character of the Mussulman races along our northwest frontier. The 'Akhûnd' of 'Swât,' and other religious leaders of that quarter, are always keeping up a 'raw,' so to speak, in the religious field. With all these and many other tokens of religious jealousy and irritation, and with the bitterness specially displayed against us by the Mussulmans in the Mutiny of 1857, it is idle to say there can be no danger of Mohammedan disaffection in India.

Sir George Campbell has not been more fortunate, perhaps, in his estimate of the religious feeling between the Mohammedans of India and their co-religionists in Turkey. He tells us in his 'Handy-Book of the Eastern Question,' p. 41, that the idea of 'any direct religious connection between the Sultan of Turkey and the Indian Mohammedans is absolutely and entirely untrue;' and that it would be quite as correct to say that the Emperor of Russia is the religious head of the English and French Christians, as to say that the Sultan was the religious head of any one of the Indian Mohammedans.

This is an *argumentum ad absurdum* with a vengeance, and if applied to the common Bengâlee Mohammedan, perhaps it might be correct, seeing that probably not one in ten of that class could repeat the 'Kulmah,' or profession of his faith, and could not reasonably be expected, under those circumstances, to know much of the Sultan of 'Roum;' but among educated and intelligent Mussulmans the Sultan is always spoken of with respect and veneration. Without going so far as to say that he is regarded as their direct religious head, we do assert that he is holden in high reverence by the better class of Mohammedans in India, and this sentiment might, through the agency of the 'Moolahs,' be made to work strongly on the uneducated classes. The fact is, that statements like those on which we have been commenting, especially when put forth by persons of some official status, and who might be supposed to have more solid grounds for their assertions, are calculated to do much mischief, both in giving our countrymen an incorrect view of the real state of the question, and in giving the Indian Mohammedans the idea that their position is altogether unappreciated in England.

We may take occasion to notice here briefly some views which have been put forth by other writers on the subject of the Mohammedan character. An article in 'Fraser's Magazine' for November 1876, reviewing Mr. Bosworth Smith's 'Mohammed and the Mohammedans,' a work of authority, and comparing the exterminating process of removing the Indians in North America, argues that if these races had been 'in subjection to the thirty millions of Mohammedans in India, instead of the thirty millions of Christians in America, the wars fought against them would have been not wars of extermination but of proselytising; the millions who were found on the continent would now be alive in their descendants, and absorbed in the national life.' This may be sentiment, but it is not history. From this writer an ordinary reader would understand that a complete amalgamation had taken place among the races in India, and that the process of Mohammedan proselytising had been a gentle influence, brought successfully to bear on the outnumbering millions of Hindoo and other creeds. But how different are the facts. The representatives of the diverse creeds in India will no more amalgamate than oil and vinegar, and, for the process of Mohammedan conversion, and the treatment of subjects of other creeds by Mussulman rulers, let the reviewer consult his History of India, and study the record of the reigns of Muhmood Ghuznevi, Balban, Ala-u-deen, Mahomed Toghluk, and others, and he may arrive at a more accurate estimate than he at present possesses of the tender method of Mohammedan proselytising and the gentle mercy of Moslem kings.

In the reign of 'Akbar' and his immediate successors, the Hindoos had, with some variations, a better time of it, and individuals of that creed were advanced to posts of trust and importance, but they were never considered by the great body of Mohammedans as other than infidels and idolaters; and after six centuries of Moslem rule, they were scarcely more 'absorbed in the national life' of their conquerors—if by that is meant their becoming a representative body in the government of the country under the Mohammedans—than they were at the first conquest. They have fared better under their more recent masters, for strong efforts have been made of late years to educate the people up to self-government.

Another writer on 'Islamism,' quoted in the same

article, Major Osborn, does not allow the British Government even this small credit. He says we have made India a 'gigantic model prison,' and her regeneration is not to be expected under British rule. He adds, 'Estimating the effects of British rule by its results on the spirits of men, we shall find that the races of India have declined in the courage and manliness which produce a vigorous nation in proportion to the period they have been subjected to the blighting influence of an alien despotism. No human power can avail to arrest the progress of decay in a people bereft of political freedom except the restitution of that freedom.' These be brave words, but unfortunately the conclusions are drawn from incorrect premises. The people have *not* declined in courage and manliness. The men who fought us in the Mutiny opposed us on more equal terms, and with better relative success, than their forefathers met the pigmy hosts of Clive and Lake; and for political freedom, when in the whole record of history have the races of India been known to possess it? Did the Hindoos enjoy political freedom under the Mohammedan Emperors I have named above? Did the Mussulman subjects themselves possess it? Any careful reader of Indian history knows that despotism pure and simple is the only form of government which that country has ever known, whether in the form of a single ruler, like 'Bâber' or 'Akhbar' on the throne of Agra, exercising his sway over countless subject states, or among the small chiefs, who aired their petty tyranny over a more limited area.

On this subject the following passage from the Arnold

Prize Essay of 1867 on the 'Mohammedan Power in India' forms a good comment on what has been advanced above. Speaking of the influence of caste on the Hindoo population, the author remarks :—'By creating groups, and not gradations in society, it prevented the play of national life. Thus the people of India remained tied to the land, and spell-bound by caste, while the dynasties and characters of their rulers changed and shifted in endless variety.' On this the author quotes in a note Buckle on civilisation. 'In India abject eternal slavery was the natural state of the great body of the people; it was the state to which they were doomed by physical laws utterly impossible to resist.' The author of the prize essay does not agree with this summary mode of dealing with the question, but considers that, when 'we reach historic times, it becomes obvious that the action of physical causes is continually modified by the action of causes having their origin in human agency;' the agency in the author's opinion being caste, as he explains in the text. These passages are quoted in support of the view that national life and political freedom have been hitherto unknown quantities in India.

Assuming, then, as it is to be feared we must, that, under present circumstances, the Mohammedans in India as a body are not cordial well-wishers to the state, we should at least be entitled to look for the loyal regard of the Hindoos for securing to them the benefits of freedom and just government; but the followers of that creed also hold aloof from us in a manner which it is difficult to account for, except from the desire for change which is inherent in all nationalities, but which is more strongly developed in the peoples of India than among other races.

Some few years ago, when, among other projects for lessening the state expenditure, it was proposed to reduce the strength of the artillery in India, Lord Napier of Magdala, who has had the experience of a lifetime in India, in protesting against the measure remarked as follows:—

'It appears to me that we never had less hold on the affections of the people than at present. The remembrance of the benefits which we conferred on the people of India that we relieved from oppression and misrule has passed away with the people of those days. The present generation only consider their present restraints and the obligations imposed on them, and the more educated and ambitious look for a larger share of emolument and influence than they now possess.' I presume that the general purport of these utterances will be allowed to be correct, even by the most sanguine. Past benefits are forgotten, and grievances of the present are rankling in their minds, while vague expectations of something turning up in the future are disturbing the whole native community. Our proceedings during the last quarter of a century are accountable in some measure, perhaps, for this unsettled state of feeling, inasmuch as we have attempted to force upon the natives of India our ideas of Western progress before there has been any attempt to prepare them for it. You cannot change the customs, the fixed habits of ages in a decade; you cannot make Oriental thought assume the form of Western ideas by a 'presto pass,' like a conjuror; and the attempt to do so has, as I think, resulted in failure. Kaye, in his 'Sepoy War,' has characterised the attempt as a 'forcing process of unwholesome rapidity;' and it well deserves the appellation. The consequence is that India has become a land of incongruities. By the side of the express train whirling through the waste at thirty or forty miles an hour, you shall see the ancient hackery (native cart), the vehicle of a period before the Cæsars, and the driver twisting his patient bullocks' tails to get two miles an hour out of them. Floating down the 'fabulosus Hydaspes,' you may behold the same kind of craft which carried Alexander toiling after the swift Western steamer; and jogging under the electric wire pants the Indian postman, carrying the mails at the extreme rate of four miles an hour.

Material discrepancies like these might not be of much account, if they did not typify moral and social incongruities of a like degree, and involving more serious consequences. We have ourselves to blame in a measure for this, as has been intimated above, from a mistaken appreciation of the receptivity of the natives of India of measures of progress and social improvement. We have been led into doing the right thing at the wrong season; but the most bitter and persistent of our enemies cannot charge us with evil intention in our endeavours to minister to the welfare of the people. The effort has been all for good, though it has failed from its premature development.

We have admitted natives as members into the

Legislative Council. We have constituted them in large numbers members of the municipal corporations of their respective townships, with the view of leading them up to self-government. We have spread the advantages of education broadcast throughout the land, have encouraged a native press, and accorded it the same freedom it possesses in our own land, in the hope of elevating the intellectual condition of the people. We have recognised (one might almost write, fostered) the religious interests of all creeds in India, to an extent unknown among subject races in other countries, and the result of all our good intentions and acts has been disheartening failure. Our want of success is to be attributed, doubtless, to the inability of the native races in India to utilise or to appreciate the means of self-improvement which we have desired to impart to them; but to determine what the causes of this incapacity may be would call for much fuller treatment than can be accorded in a brief summary like this. It can only be generally stated here, that Oriental human nature is not Anglo-Saxon human nature, and that the national character of the latter, which it has taken centuries to form and mature, may hardly be developed in an Indian race in five and twenty years.

But it may be asked, Has not our example had some effect? Has not the contact of the natives with us been productive of some material improvement among them? The Persian poet 'Sâdi' has a pretty fable, 'The Rose and the Grass.' The latter, on being reproached with its insignificance and worthlessness as compared with the flower, pleads that it has been tied up with the rose, and has derived some of its sweetness. It would be a happy thing for both races if this might be urged with truth by our Indian fellow-subjects. Not that our example has been always of so high a character as might have been desired, but still we might claim a modicum of gratitude from the people of India for much good in intention, and for a considerable measure of benefits actually conferred. Is there any significance in the fact that there is no word for gratitude in the Hindostanee language? Some results of our endeavour to improve and educate the people will be considered further on.

CHAPTER XIII.

Relation of native soldiers with their officers — Of civil officers and ryots — Unsettled state of feeling in India — Social relations between Europeans and natives — Importance of union among English in India — Present want of esprit de corps — Russian movements in Central Asia, and their effect in India.

IN all discussions of Indian affairs the army will necessarily occupy an important position, and it may not be out of place here, perhaps, to consider the present relations of the native soldiery with their officers. Formerly an officer rose in the regiment he was first posted to—travelled from cadet to colonel in the same vehicle—held charge probably of the same company for ten or fifteen years—knew the family history of all his men, and was looked up to and confided in by them as their natural protector. *Now* officers are shifted about from regiment to regiment; there are, properly speaking, no company officers under the present system. The accounts, internal economy, and management of the regiment (subject of course to the commanding officer) are vested in the two officers commanding the 'wings,' who cannot of course be expected to attain the same intimate knowledge of half a regiment as a company officer could of his charge under the old régime, setting aside their constant liability to be shifted to another regiment on promotion or for acting appointments. It is true that the existence of these ties between the native soldier and his officer did not prevent the breaking out of the Mutiny, but it should be remembered that some time before that the old régime had received a severe shock from the inauguration of the centralisation system, whereby the powers of commanding officers had been grievously curtailed, and the influence of company officers sensibly weakened, and it seems highly probable that the hasty introduction of novelties, the pressure of unseasonable progress from high quarters, have to answer in great measure for the outbreak of the insurrection.

Nor are the present relations of the civil officers with the people of a more satisfactory character. Formerly civil officers moved about their districts making themselves acquainted with the habits of the people, their customs, and the social progress of the village communities. Now, for the most part, the officers are so hampered with office-work, that they have little leisure for making these social progresses; or, if they have, a line has been drawn so hard and fast by the modern system, that the old friendly intercourse between the district officers and their people is now almost impossible. We have quoted above the admission of the Government that officers on the frontier are so harassed with office-work that they are unable to pay proper attention to that which should be their principal duty—cultivating friendly relations with the border chiefs—and this applies with twofold force to the officers in charge of the more central districts. A certain latitude is allowed to frontier officers, both as regards law (not justice) and routine, but from the Indus to the Beas the incubus of officialdom and statistics reigns supreme, and to add to the burden of the officers of those regions, almost every petty case in court is now represented by a pleader, whereby the course of a suit is often hopelessly protracted, the officer's time wasted, and litigation unnecessarily increased. On the latter point there will be more to say presently. It would seem that a civil officer's merits now are estimated by his averages of legal work performed, and by the polish put on his civil and criminal judgments, and not by his power as an administrator or by his success in ruling men. The effect of all this appears to be, that a state of unrest has been created throughout the land.

The natives are taking, like the Athenians of old, to asking τὶ καινὸν λέγεται; and one might answer in the spirit of Demosthenes, 'What can be newer than that a foreign army, unfriendly in intent, if not yet in act, is within a few days' march of the gates of India!' The gossip of the bazaar embraces now more dangerous elements than the price of grain or the domestic concerns of men's neighbours. This unsettled condition has been noticed on former occasions when stirring events have been occurring on the frontier. Thus, with regard to the Persian siege of Herât and the Affghan war of 1838–42, Kaye writes, 'In our own provinces these rumours of mighty movements in the countries of the north-west disquieted the native mind. There was an uneasy, restless feeling among all classes, scarcely amounting to disaffection, and perhaps best to be described as a state of ignorant expectancy—a looking outward in the belief of some coming change, the nature of which no one clearly understood.'

Rawlinson's 'England and Russia in Central Asia' notices this disturbing influence, and anticipates its increase as the Russians advance. It should be a humiliating reflection to our proud Anglo-Saxon temperament, that after a century of English government, there has been so little approach of the governed towards the rulers, that the original chasm created by the difference of creed, race, and habits has not been decreased; that we to all intents and purposes govern India by the sword as much as we did in the days of Clive, and that we owe our position in the country to the disunion of the races which inhabit it. But we are not solely, if principally, to blame in this matter. It has been the fashion among recent writers, both in India and England, to attribute the present unsatisfactory state of our relations with the natives of India to our want of cordiality, and the absence of all endeavour on our part to ingratiate ourselves with them. The roughness and hauteur of the Anglo-Saxon temperament have been assigned as the causes of this coldness and indifference, and to a certain extent it must be admitted that there are grounds for the charge. The treatment of natives by officers of English regiments, for instance, has often been unfavourably commented on; and though it may be hoped that there has been a change for the better of late years in this respect, there is still too much aversion entertained, and sometimes forcibly displayed, on the part of English officers towards 'niggers,' under which impalatable term natives of all degrees in India are commonly classified by them.

It is not unnatural that officers of English regiments should imbibe unfavourable impressions of the natives, as they are for the most part brought into contact with only the least attractive specimens of the class. Moreover, the sojourn of English regiments in India is very uncertain, and often for a very brief period, so that the officers have no inducement to study the language, without a knowledge of which it is of course impossible to arrive at any just estimate of the character of the people. It may be fairly assumed that the treatment of natives above referred to proceeds rather from thoughtlessness and indifference than from any actively hostile feeling or dislike on the part of European officers towards the people; and it is probable that if the military authorities were to let it be clearly understood that a rude and overbearing treatment of the natives would be regarded with grave displeasure at headquarters, the effect would be to secure a more courteous, if not a more cordial attitude towards them. But although these unsatisfactory sentiments, as regards the natives of the country, may exist on the part of the officers, they are not always, perhaps not generally, shared by the men of English regiments. In former times the most cordial feelings have been known to prevail between British soldiers and Sepoys. It was a common thing for men of the native regiments to carry carefully and tenderly to barracks any British soldiers whom they met with unable to find their way there by themselves, and when British and native regiments had been quartered together for any length of time, the friendliness between the British soldier and 'Johnny,' as they called the Sepoy, was remarkable.

In the Affghanistan campaign, and especially at Jellâlabad, the cordiality which subsisted between these two very opposite representatives of the British army is a matter of history, and Indian readers will doubtless remember the well-known story of the Sepoys, when the troops were on short rations, making over the rice to the English soldiers, and contenting themselves with the water in which it had been boiled, saying that their European brethren in arms required the solid food more than they did. It is, of course, desirable that these feelings should be encouraged to the utmost, but the difficulties are greater than in former years. The duration of British regiments' employment in India has been reduced from twenty to ten years, and the term of individual service has been materially curtailed, so that time is not allowed for the growth of a good understanding between English soldiers and Sepoys. A local European army afforded the most favourable conditions for the development of these friendly feelings between the two races, and this is one of the many powerful arguments which might be advanced in favour of that most valuable instrument, so heedlessly, as many think, cast aside after the Mutiny. But after all has been urged of our backwardness in encouraging friendly sentiments towards

L

the natives of India, there is something to be said on
the other part, and that is, that the races of India, in
their present stage of development, will not, perhaps
cannot, meet us half-way. While the bigotry of the
Mohammedan creed maintains its present grasp upon
the followers of that religion, and so long as the caste
exclusiveness of the Hindoos holds its sway, there is a
social barrier between us which can never be entirely
overpassed. It is perhaps a low view to take of a
great social and religious question, but so long as a man
will neither eat nor drink with you, any real social
rapprochement between that individual and yourself is
hopeless. It is true that some of the more enlightened
Mohammedans will sit with us at table, and acknow-
ledge that we are entitled to some religious consideration, recognising us, according to the teaching of the
'Korân,' as 'Ahul-i-Kitâb,' people having a revealed
religion. But the number of the liberal Mohammedans
is very very few, and even they are more or less
influenced by the vast narrow-minded majority, who,
as has been said elsewhere, are strongly impregnated
with the prejudices of their Hindoo compatriots, and
hence their belief forms a mosaic, of which bigotry,
ignorance, and caste are the chief constituent parts.
The caste of the Hindoo appears at first to be a more
serious obstacle to social intimacy than the intolerance
of the other religionists. As to eating or drinking with
you, a high-caste Hindoo would sooner die; if you pass
near the small enclosure where he cooks his food, the
bread is defiled and cast to the dogs; if you drink out of
any vessel belonging to him, it is destroyed forthwith.

But there is more hope of overcoming a prejudice which is partly social and partly religious, than there is of softening a hatred which is based on an idea of religious superiority and a sense of religious injury.

The 'Brahmo-Somâj' movement shows that the power of Hindooism is being gradually undermined by the spread of civilisation and the diffusion of general knowledge, but no signs are yet visible of a change in the spirit of Mohammedanism. With the latter, reformers, instead of striking, as the 'Brahmo-Somâj' separatists have done, at the very root of the faith in which they were nurtured, intensify the spirit while they would modify the ritual of the parent creed.

The 'Wahâbees,' for instance, would abolish all the quasi-idolatrous practices which have crept into the religion of 'Islâm,' such as the deifying of Mohammed, decorating the tombs of saints, pilgrimages, and so forth, but for the enforcement of the tenets of the faith, according to their interpretation of them, you could find no sterner bigots. They are *plus arabe qu'en arabie.* Let us hope, however, that time and reflection may bring our Mussulman subjects to a right appreciation of our conduct and intentions towards them. These may contrast favourably, at any rate, with the course pursued by the other European conquerors across the Oxus. We, at least, have not erred on the side of persecution, nor have we adopted as our motto, as the Muscovites appear to have done, the converse of St. Bernard's advice to the Pope, *Aggredere eos, non verbo, sed ferro!*

It may be fairly claimed in our favour that civil

officers, military officers with native regiments, and others whose employments entail a constant association with the natives, do endeavour, in a greater or less degree, according to temperament and opportunity, to cultivate friendly relations with them, and cordial intimacies not rarely follow. It is, therefore, desirable that facilities should be afforded, to the civil officers especially, for maintaining freely social intercourse with those whose interests they are appointed to superintend, and to this end a relaxing of the present official strain is most advisable.

Thus much has been said to show, that though we stand accountable for a considerable degree of blame in the matter of conciliation towards the people, the fault is not altogether on our side. Both parties require educating, ourselves to a greater readiness to offer, and the natives to more willingness to accept, the invitation to a better understanding, and a more cordial connection between the two races. And as a nearer approach to union with the native races is a consummation much to be desired, it is of perhaps still greater moment that the representatives of the governing class should be thoroughly and heartily at one among themselves. The proverb that 'unity is strength' found its full confirmation in the early period of the annexation of the Punjaub, and during the severest crisis we have ever passed through in India, the revolt of 1857. Kaye writes thus on the subject: 'The chief officers of the Punjaub were bound together, not merely by the excitement of a common object. The bonds of a common affection were equally strong within them, and each was eager to express his admiration of the good deed of another. There may have been good-fellowship in other provinces, but in none was there such fellowship as this' ("Sepoy War," ii. 487). One can hardly venture to say that that feeling exists now, at any rate to the same extent as formerly. All the old associations are broken up, and no attempt has been made to renew them.

The men who helped to win and first managed the Punjaub are nearly all gone, and with them have vanished for the most part the old 'Sikh' chiefs, who met us bravely first sword in hand, and helped us nobly afterwards with their counsel and influence. The new school of officials has neither the old associations to fall back upon, the ancient 'Sikh' counsellors to look to for help, nor have they the same freedom of action that the old officers had. The present race of officials is fettered by codes and formalities, bound as it were hand and foot with red tape. They lack, moreover, the bond of 'good-fellowship' which Kaye speaks of, inasmuch as they have not passed through the same stirring events, nor experienced the community of danger, which brought the old Punjaubees together, and to judge from their writings, their sentiments towards their brother officials are much the same as we might expect from the officials in a Government department at home looking out for promotion. It is the fashion in India nowadays to sneer at the idea of patriarchal government, the rule of social regard as contrasted with government by regulation. It is stated to be an anachronism. May be so, as read in the aspect of Western progress, but it is beyond doubt better suited to Oriental human nature in its present state of development than the overwrought system now obtaining; and it possessed one great advantage at least over the present order of things, that the bundle of faggots was united and entire, whereas now it is a case of each stick for himself! There is now in India but little remainder of the old *esprit de corps*, or whatever you like to call the sentiment which binds a body of men together, gives each a common interest in the other, and looks to the general good rather than to the selfish aggrandisement of the individual. Our want of concord at home may be an important feature when the pressure comes from abroad, and that such pressure is not far distant few but the wilfully blind are prepared to doubt. Whatever the 'masterly inactives' may say, the movements of Russia in Central Asia and her future designs are becoming daily more discussed in India, both among the educated classes and in the gossip of the bazaar; and, at the risk of being charged with 'Russophoby,' we shall venture to offer a few remarks on the subject. And at the outset it may be observed, that instead of applying the term 'Russophobists' to those who, like Sir H. Rawlinson and other eminent men, would warn the country against the *laissez aller* policy of the 'inactivity' school, the saddle should be shifted to the back of the right quadruped. 'Russophoby' is a misnomer as applied to those who foresee the danger which threatens in allowing the Russians to advance unquestioned on all sides of our Indian dominions, and who have the courage to grasp the nettle at once. Rather does the term apply to those who would let the question 'slide' from real fear to grapple with it, content only that the evil should not happen in their day; for this, setting aside the garnish of belief in the honest (?) intentions of Russia, the advantages of civilising the nations of Central Asia and so forth, this is the real and selfish intent of the 'inactivity' policy. It is by no means intended to assert that all the supporters of this policy are actuated by the same selfish motives. No one would charge Lord Lawrence, for instance, with selfishness or fear as regards his political opinions; but excessive caution in important affairs, and, if I may so term it, a persistent course of postponement of action, gives a complexion of timidity to such a policy, even if it be not really inherent in it.

> 'The native hue of resolution
> Is sicklied o'er with the pale cast of thought,
> And deeds and enterprises of great pith and moment
> Become awry, and lose the name of action.'

The view taken, however, by the majority of the cautious party appears to be this: The difficulty cannot present itself for years to come; the present state of affairs will last our time; let posterity look out for itself. Or, to borrow one of the rounded periods of the 'Times,' 'They prefer the policy of waiting upon events to the policy of controlling them.' It would not be difficult to show from the writings of these—what shall we call them—'Russophiles,' that this is the real meaning of the 'inactivity' policy. Grant Duff, who we suppose may be considered an authoritative exponent of these views, tells us in his 'Notes of an Indian Journey,' that 'Russia has done nothing in Central Asia which she had not a perfect right to do as far as we are concerned. But as to how far she may have made imprudent statements as to what she meant and did not mean to do, that is a matter on which I express no opinion.'

But that is the very matter in question. How far we allowed ourselves to be bamboozled by Russia as to her progress in Central Asia by statements which Mr. Duff calls imprudent, but which common men would term wilfully deceitful, in the past, and how far we are going to allow ourselves to be led by the nose by similar 'imprudent' manifestoes in the future, is just the point on which the question of policy hinges, and on this, with characteristic 'inactivity,' the author leaves us entirely in the dark. Take the utterances of another author and representative of this school, a writer in the 'Fortnightly Review,' now known as the late Mr. Wyllie, formerly an Under-Secretary in the Indian Foreign Office. In the 'Fortnightly Review' of December 1869, General Jacob's proposal to occupy Quettah was treated with much contumely. The plan was opposed, according to Mr. Wyllie, by Lord Lawrence, then Governor-General, on the score of expense, possible jealousy of Persia, and because it might be done at some future time (the 'inactive' rule of faith). Lord Lawrence was supported, Mr. Wyllie states, by Sir W. Mansfield, then Commander-in-chief, and by Sir H. Durand; by the former chiefly on the score of expense.

The proposal originated by General Jacob and supported by Sir Bartle Frere, and, therefore, one would suppose, entitled to some sort of respect, is, Mr. Wyllie pertly remarks in 1869, 'still vigorous in the vitality of popular error.' The 'popular error' has lived so strongly, that the advance to Quettah is an accomplished fact; the railway to the mouth of the Bolan Pass and the road through it are matters only of time, and the occupation of Candahar and Herât depends only, we trust, on the movements of Russia.

When General Jacob's plan was negatived, the Russians had not reached 'Khiva.' *Now* they have absorbed the greater portion of that state, and 'Ferghâna' has become a Russian province—'Ferghâna,' from whence 'Bâber' sallied to conquer India. *Absit omen.*

CHAPTER XIV.

*Further remarks on Russian movements in Central Asia—
State of feeling among certain native chiefs in India—The
native press of India—Reforms required in taxation—Police
—Law—Army—Responsibilities of England to India—
Conclusion.*

Is it possible to doubt any longer with what intent
Russia is strengthening herself in Central Asia? Can
human credulity extend so far as to believe that they
are there for the purpose of bettering the condition of
the people of those parts, of evangelising the Khanates?
Surely the time for all this is gone by. After the
revelations of Schuyler and M'Gahan, both of them
'Russophiles' (to judge from their subsequent writings,
at least), of what Russian proselytising really means,
submission or the sword, it is impossible for any one to
continue in the belief that Russia has only the welfare
of the people at heart in extending her dominions to
the 'Oxus.' What remains? Lord Lawrence admits
that Russia can derive no benefit from the occupation
of Turkestan. He says, 'According to the best authorities, such as Schuyler and M'Gahan, Russia gains
no real profit from the subjugation of the Khanates
of Turkestan; those countries do not pay the expense

of the occupation, and the commercial advantages therefrom are insignificant, if we bear in mind that a good deal of commerce which exists would still accrue to her even if Russia ceased to be the dominant power.' Why is she there then? I do not know that a stronger argument could be adduced as to what *we* believe to be the intentions of Russia than these remarks from the pen of a principal supporter of the 'masterly inactivity' policy.

Lord Lawrence goes on to dilate on the difficulties of the country for an invading army, and instances the hardships encountered by Peroffsky in 1839, and by Kauffman, but he does not see, apparently, how these very circumstances tell against the views of his party, that Russia has no designs upon India; for why should these difficulties have been encountered again and again if the Russians' only object was to occupy a country confessedly profitless to them? Schuyler (the quotation is from the 'Fortnightly Review' of March 1870) estimates the money loss by 'Turkestan' at the time he writes at £2,000,000; Terentyeff admits a deficit of £2,800,000 between 1868 and 1877. The difficulties above enumerated are not likely to be experienced again. The navigation of the Oxus is being opened rapidly, and the main road from Orenberg to Tashkend is doubtless progressing apace, to be followed at no very distant period by a railway, and a late report informs us that telegraphic communication is complete between 'Ferghâna' and St. Petersburg. Lastly, the railway between 'Perm' and 'Ekaterinburg,' on the *eastern* side of the Ural Mountains, has been formally opened, and the St. Petersburg papers inform us, 'The country beyond Ekaterinburg is being surveyed for the projected line to Central Asia.'

When the next move in advance will be made it is of course idle to speculate. It may depend in some measure, perhaps, on the advantages or otherwise which may accrue to Russia from the present war, but we may safely reckon that another decade will bring the Sepoy and the Cossack into much closer proximity than they are at present. For our external preparation in the present, the occupation of 'Quettah' in force, and the improvement of the communication therewith, would perhaps suffice. For our strength internally we must look to good government, for the first means used by our wily enemy will be the stirring up of disaffection among the natives of India, a process which has been begun probably long since, but which will gather strength as his state of preparedness advances. Rumours are strong even now of disaffection among some of our great feudatory chiefs, who maintain, in more than one instance, a far larger number of troops than their requirements can possibly justify. In the opinion of many, we have made a great mistake in our late treatment of these chiefs; stars, grand crosses, generals' rank, &c., have been showered upon them, and fulsome flattery has been added. Oriental human nature cannot stand such treatment, and the consequence is, that, like children, they are spoilt. As their compatriots would say, they are become 'hawa-been,' lookers at the wind, or, as we might term it, they have their noses in the air. Whether it be true or not that some of these parties have been visited and tampered with by Russian agents, as report goes, it is certain that some few of them have shown by their conduct lately that their awe and respect for the dominant power are greatly on the wane. This is a matter to be carefully looked to, for when the pressure comes, our difficulties will be greater from within than from without.

If we can reckon then as now upon the regard of the 'Sikhs' and other sects from whom we draw our soldiers, we may calculate on giving a good account of any Russian army which attempts to force the passes in Affghanistan, but unless we have a contented people behind us, our strength at the point of contact with an invading force will avail us nothing. Above all, the land wants rest, and for some years past there has been too much turmoil and excitement, royal progresses, imperial proclamations, viceregal durbars, and pageants, following one another with dangerous rapidity, and the advantage of them is open to grave question. The expense they put the native chiefs to and the heartburnings they engender outweigh greatly, it is to be feared, any profit which might be derived from ministering to the supposed native fondness for pomp and spectacle. A native chief likes display when he is the principal figure in the show, but when he is hustled among a hundred others, some of whom probably make a better show than himself, his *amour propre* is hurt, and disgust and dissatisfaction are the only sentiments he carries away with him. This is known to have been the case with 'Scindia,' who turned sulky at some fancied slight at one of these pageants, and has not hesitated to show his temper since by acts of discourtesy and rudeness to high officials in India. This is one of the individuals also who is keeping up an army far in excess of his requirements, and he probably would be, or is, one of the first objects of Russian intrigue.

Another ready-made agent for the furtherance of Russian schemes will be found in the native newspapers, to which, following our usual course of thrusting prematurely Western institutions on Oriental habits, we have accorded the freedom of the press, and an edifying use has been made of this liberty. Extracts from the native journals were published in one of the London morning papers not long since, teeming with abuse of the Government of India; but these specimens are mild to what are sometimes met with in the vernacular newspapers. This is another specimen of the unfitness of things in India. We have prematurely accorded to a narrow-minded Oriental people a boon which some countries in Europe even are not supposed to be fit for, and who can wonder that it has been abused. Freedom of the press requires a sound public opinion to balance it, and this does not exist in India in any shape. The consequence has been, that our attempt to treat the natives of India as an enlightened community has only had the effect of letting loose a continual stream of abuse on all that is English, and instead of instructing and elevating public opinion, the vernacular press is only concerned with raising disaffection among the people.

> ' Amphora cœpit
> Institui, currente rota cur urceus exit ? '

The vase is ever turning out a pitcher on our hands. Such is the history of most of our experiments in India of late years. What is to be done ? It requires a master-hand to deal with the difficulties of the situation now.

'O for one hour of Wallace wight!' O for a brief season of the great Proconsul, Lord Dalhousie, to take the helm while the bark is among the breakers! We may not look upon his like again, I fear, but let us hope that, with God's help, the necessity may produce the man ere long, one strong of will and firm of purpose, who shall hold his course unswayed by disturbing counsels of Indian or English advisers—one who will suffer the labouring land to rest awhile and recover its power. There is more than enough work for all departments in repairing and restoring, without resorting to sensational legislation and to expensive and useless exhibitions. The system of taxation throughout the country requires a thorough supervision and readjustment. The police system calls for searching inquiry and remodelling of the organisation generally, if we may trust the constant complaints against the force which appear in the Indian papers. The law codes require modification, as do the rules of business for the civil courts, for litigation is becoming the curse of the land. In the fifth and sixth years after the annexation of the Punjaub, 1854-55, the number of civil suits instituted averaged 60,800 per annum. In the following decade, 1864-65, the number of civil suits instituted respectively was 103,700, and 139,400; and in 1873–74, the totals had reached 221,850 and 230,650, with an ever-upward tendency. This unhappy spirit of litigation has been fostered by the increased facilities afforded for resort to the law courts, the multiplication of courts of appeal, whereby a suitor gets three or four chances of a favourable decision of his claim instead of one, and perhaps above all, by the great increase in the number of pleaders, who now throng (one might write infest) the law courts. It is true that an attempt is made to regulate the admission of advocates by examination tests, and by empowering the District officers to bar persons of bad character; but the law examination is comparatively an easy one, and it is almost impossible for an officer to arrive at anything like a correct estimate of a native candidate's character unless there is something flagrant or notorious against him. The consequence is that the courts are flooded with pleaders of all sorts, Europeans, half-castes, and natives, very few unfortunately of the first named. Among the others, there are many needy and unprincipled adventurers, who live on their neighbours' quarrels, and whose object of course it is to foment litigation to the uttermost. Not long ago it was the practice of some of these so-called lawyers to keep 'touts,' whose business it was to waylay agriculturists and others coming to the courts and bring them to their employer, who of course vaunted his own talents and influence, and promised a speedy and victorious termination to the suit. The unhappy 'ryots' were often thus deluded, and it would not rarely happen that, instead of winning or losing a comparatively inexpensive suit, which he might have done if he had kept clear of the pleader's clutches, the unfortunate victim has been led on from court to court, original and appeal, and at the end of the business, what with costs and pleader's fees, has returned home with little more than the coat to his back. This practice of 'touting' became so glaring and abominable, that the chief court was obliged to interfere, and there is reason to believe that it is not conducted now in so barefaced a manner as formerly, though it is to be feared that this trade is still carried on, and it must of course tell greatly against the popularity of the courts.

Taxation is perhaps the most fertile cause of discontent among the Hindoos, as they constitute the main body of urban taxpayers. The land tax, which affects only the rural communities, is as a rule fairly and equitably distributed, and its realisation can afford no reasonable grounds for dissatisfaction. But this source of revenue, the backbone of Indian finance, does not admit at present of much further expansion, and in the increased expenditure which has been entailed of late years by the requirements of the Public Works Department, the support of the Home administration, and by the ever-increasing loss by exchange, it has become necessary to resort to other forms of taxation to meet the deficiencies caused by this drain on the resources of the country. The income tax was tried first, and after a brief course was abolished as a failure. It was not only most unpalatable to the people in consequence of the inquisitorial process by which it was accompanied, but it failed to reach, in any appreciable degree, the class for which it was intended, namely, the wealthy among the urban population, a body from which the Government may most legitimately demand assistance in supplementing the revenues of the country. At present this class pays next to nothing in the way of taxation, and the cesses by which they were formerly made to contribute indirectly to the state revenues, such as house taxes, town dues, and so forth, having been abrogated, or reduced to such an extent as barely to provide for the expense of each municipality, the singular spectacle is presented of the wealthiest portion of the nation escaping the burden of taxation, which has therefore to be borne by the poorer members of the community. The recent introduction of a trade tax appears to have created nearly as unfavourable an impression as the income tax, inasmuch as it shares some of the most obnoxious features of the latter, especially the official inquiry into sources of income, and the Finance Minister must be at his wit's end how to achieve the impossible, in other words, to raise money in a popular way.

The subject is too vast to discuss in these pages. All that can be said is, that taxation which is general in its incidence is more popular with, or rather less obnoxious to, the people than that which involves personal inquiry like the income tax. Take the *octroi* for instance. The last year's collection of this cess in its original form in the Punjaub amounted to R.20.11.074. Its substitute or successor, the income tax, realised for the first six months of the ensuing year R.3996.74, the annual total not amounting to half the amount of the *octroi*. In the report announcing these results it was added, that 'in every town there is a large party of traders who would hail with gladness the revival of the *octroi.*' If we must have additional taxation, it is surely better to let it assume a form which is familiar, and, as far as any scheme of taxation can be, popular with the community, rather than adhere to systems which have only the doubtful recommendation of their Western parentage. If the trade tax is to be maintained at all hazards, it is to be hoped that the unpopular measure of official scrutiny for the purpose of determining the amount of individual incomes may be avoided. At the time of the imposition of the income tax in the Punjaub, the practice was often resorted to of making the trades and guilds assess the members of their respective communities, and pay the amount for each guild in a lump sum, a reasonable average being of course assigned, and this process rendered the dreaded official inquiry unnecessary. The question of retrenchment affords almost as wide a scope for the powers of a financier as that of the distribution of taxation. The subject of reduction of expenditure engages deeply the attention of the Indian Government, and it is to be hoped the English branch of the administration also; for the loss of millions annually from the single item of exchange forms a burden which the revenues of India in their present inelastic condition cannot fairly be expected to support.

It remains to consider, lastly, the army, which, since the amalgamation in 1861, or rather since the Mutiny, has been made the subject of constant experiment, like the Public Works Department. We do not now allude to the 'muddle,' as it has been generally called, in the way of regulating promotion, retirement, and so forth, which the authors of the amalgamation scheme landed themselves in, but to the more important questions of the reorganisation of the native army and the abolition of the local European force. Public opinion has long since declared itself on the first point, that the change was injudicious, 'and the powers that be' appear to be slowly coming to the same conclusion. If the *efficiency* of the native army is to be considered, the argument for an increased number of European officers does not admit of question, especially in the not very remote contingency of our being brought into contact with a European power. The expense is another matter, but the difficulty requires to be boldly and promptly faced.

On the subject of the abolition of the local European army one might write volumes. At the Mutiny we had a body of 9,000 or 10,000 men, ready to hand, used to the country, and content to dwell in it; and ordinary mortals would have thought that the best policy would have been to extend and increase this valuable agency; but it was heedlessly sacrificed to the passion for uniformity which had then taken possession of our rulers and their advisers. The advantages of a local European army have been often brought to notice, and independently of the benefit of having a body of men whose interests would be bound up in service in India, they might be utilised also for introducing a system of military colonisation in the country. The subject is a vast one, but it is well deserving of attentive consideration. The land is there in abundance, the climate of the Himalayas is perfection, and what the advantage would be of having bodies of European military colonists to furnish a reserve force in case of necessity, goes without saying. We need only glance at the immense relief which the measure would give to the home army.

A word in conclusion as to our responsibilities in India. Not very long ago the common saying was, that when we quitted India, the only traces of our occupation which we should leave behind us would be broken beer bottles. This would hardly hold good now as regards material relics, for there are some grand monuments in shape of railways, bridges, churches, law courts, and so forth, but as touching our moral remains, it is open to doubt if the situation is much improved within the last quarter of a century.

Our system of education so far has resulted only in the production of 'Young Bengal' and similar abortions. Among the great majority of the people, education is only regarded as a means of obtaining a livelihood, either by employment in the Government service, or by qualifying for a pleader's certificate, or the like, and that object once attained, all care for further improvement is cast to the winds; and as for education ever being looked upon as a principal means of elevating the mind and moral character, that among Indian youth is a vain delusion. If such has been the result of our system of literary education, what of the higher form of teaching by example?

We believe that until later years the natives of India have regarded their European masters as upright and honourable men so far as moral character was concerned.

They knew that, as a rule, the English judges were incorruptible, and that the word of an English officer might be accepted as an unfailing guarantee for truth. But it is to be feared that our national character has within the last few years descended from that high pedestal in the native's estimation. Not that there has been any change in the character of English officers and gentlemen in India—heaven forbid!—but a class of Europeans, some of them of the adventurer type, which did not exist in old time, has come between the official class and the natives of India, with whom the latter are now brought into more immediate contact, and from whom, it is to be feared, they form in great measure their estimate of English character. As regards our religious example, it does not stand very high in the eyes of either Hindoos or Mohammedans. Some twenty or thirty years ago the natives used to say that the only way in which the Sahib's *burra din* (great or holy day) was recognisable was by the waving of the flag, alluding to the custom of hoisting the ensign on Sunday. This reproach cannot hold good now, for there is a church, usually well attended, at every important station, and, so far as externals go, we may say that we are better than our predecessors; but it is a question whether we have, any more than they, taken our proper stand as regards the religion we profess. It is one thing to abstain from using Government influence for the propagation of one's faith; it is another to shrink from boldly professing that faith for fear of being misunderstood by Mohammedans and heathen. The latter has been the line almost universally adopted by the Indian Government. In 1799, fearful of too active a profession of the Christian faith, the Government of the day compelled Carey, who had come to Calcutta to work as a missionary, to leave the country, when he found shelter in the Danish mission at Serampoor. A little later, two Baptist missionaries who had come to assist Carey were ordered to re-embark at once. One of them went to Burmah, and originated the mission to the 'Kârens,' which has resulted in the conversion of a whole race, no less than 30,000 of them having embraced the Christian faith. In this instance it might be said that God made the fears of the Government an instrument for spreading the knowledge of the Gospel; but it is little credit to a state calling itself Christian that the benefits which have accrued have been in despite of it. Of course the argument on the other side is, that it behoves a Government ruling over people of other creeds to be very careful not to offend their prejudices, or hinder them in the observance of their respective religions. Quite so; but this course is by no means incompatible with a frank and bold assertion of the religion we profess ourselves; and we believe, and the opinion has been expressed by many whose judgment 'cries in the top of ours,' that such an unfearing bearing would carry with it more weight and more respect, the heathen themselves being our judges, than the halting, feeble course we have too long pursued. Was it by a kind of judicial retribution that, after all our concessions to native prejudices, the Mutiny of 1857 should have been brought about by a religious cry, and that of so preposterous a nature, that we were going to work the conversion of the people by pig's fat? But while, on the one hand, anything like missionary enterprise is looked upon with suspicion and distrust, the institutions of the Hindoo and Mohammedan creeds receive something like ten millions sterling as religious endowment from the state. This has been brought to notice lately in rather an amusing manner. A petition has recently been got up by what is termed the 'Indian Disestablishment Society' ('Young Bengal' again), praying that the £150,000 which is spent annually on Church Establishment in India may be discontinued, the said grant being contrary to the terms of Her Majesty's proclamation after the Mutiny, that none of Her Majesty's subjects should be 'in any wise favoured by reason of their religious faith and observance.' A counter-petition of the 'Indian Religious Equality Society' urges, on the other side, that the Hindoo and Mohammedan subjects of Her Majesty enjoy for the endowment of their religious institutions no less a sum than ten millions sterling, paid from the state revenues, while Her Majesty's Christian subjects receive a much less relative sum for the support of their religion, and this treatment of the latter is contrary to Her Majesty's proclamation, that none shall be favoured by reason of their religious faith and observances. The 'Religious Equality Society' appears to have the best of the argument.

It is hardly too much to say, that if bygone Governments in India had been as staunch in the avowal of their own faith as they have been careful of the interests of the Hindoo and Mohammedan religions, we might have been spared many complications, and have held a much

CONCLUSION.

higher position in the eyes of the people than we do at present.

The reader must judge from what has gone before how far we have fulfilled our responsibilities to India. It may be thought, perhaps, that the view taken of our position in the preceding pages is too gloomy. To this it can only be replied, that it is the 'custom of the English nation' to show the worst side of everything connected with its own interests, to 'take notes of all the holes in all our coats, and prent them,' without favour or affection. If we were writing as Russians or as Frenchmen, the account would be of the most roseate hue—our administration of justice, our equitable assessment of the land revenue, the entire freedom of the people, the liberal state support of native religious institutions, the widely-spread system of education, these and other laudable elements in the administration would be adduced by a Muscovite author to prove the excellence of the government, and with justice; only he would leave out of the catalogue all the defects which might interfere with the general happy effect. Our system, the direct contrary to this, is the honestest, and may possibly be the wisest plan, and in that belief we do not hesitate to point straight at blots which may mar an otherwise fair picture. Those who have the means of acquiring a knowledge of the inner bearings of Indian politics (which none but an observant resident can do who depends on his own judgment, and not on vague chatter and hearsay) are of opinion that the state of feeling among the natives is in a dangerous phase at present, and that very much depends upon the rulers of the land during the next few years, whether by a wise and steady course of administration they can succeed in calming the restless and inflammable spirit which now appears to pervade Indian native society, and direct it into the path of legitimate progress and development, in which case we need fear no external foes; or if, ignoring the signs of the times, our governors allow this 'state of ignorant expectancy' to gain strength, plunge India once more into the vortex of revolt, and render her and ourselves an easy prey to the far-sighted vulture, now biding his time in the deserts of Turkestan.

POSTSCRIPT.

Events march rapidly nowadays. Since the conclusion of this work the Government of India has found it necessary to curb the license of the native press by special enactment. The appointment of a Commissioner for the North-West Frontier has formed the subject of frequent reference between the Indian and Home Administrations. Turkey in Europe has almost ceased to be, and Turkey in Asia is in little better plight. All these subjects have been treated of in these pages in the aspect they presented at the time of writing, but as the object of the work has not been affected by what has occurred, no alteration has been made in the text.

THE END.

PRINTED BY BALLANTYNE, HANSON AND CO.
EDINBURGH AND LONDON.

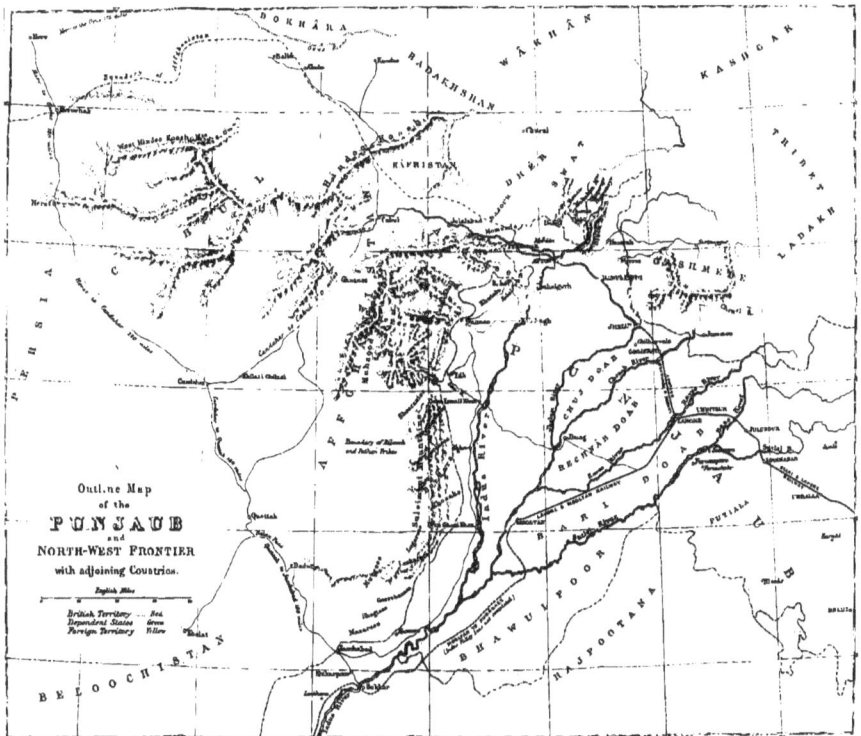

A LIST OF

KEGAN PAUL AND CO.'S

PUBLICATIONS.

1, *Paternoster Square, London.*

A LIST OF
C. KEGAN PAUL AND CO.'S PUBLICATIONS.

ABBEY (Henry).
Ballads of Good Deeds, and Other Verses. Fcap. 8vo. Cloth gilt, price 5s.

ABDULLA (Hakayit).
Autobiography of a Malay Munshi. Translated by J. T. Thomson, F.R.G.S. With Photo-lithograph Page of Abdulla's MS. Post 8vo. Cloth, price 12s.

ADAMS (A. L.), M.A., M.B., F.R.S., F.G.S.
Field and Forest Rambles of a Naturalist in New Brunswick. With Notes and Observations on the Natural History of Eastern Canada. Illustrated. 8vo. Cloth, price 14s.

ADAMS (F. O.), F.R.G.S.
The History of Japan. From the Earliest Period to the Present Time. New Edition, revised. 2 volumes. Demy 8vo. Cloth, price 21s. each. With Maps and Plans.

ADAMS (W. D.).
Lyrics of Love, from Shakespeare to Tennyson. Selected and arranged by. Fcap. 8vo. Cloth extra, gilt edges, price 3s. 6d.
Also, a Cheap Edition. Fcap. 8vo. Cloth, price 2s. 6d.

ADAMS (John), M.A.
St. Malo's Quest, and other Poems. Fcap. 8vo. Cloth, 5s.

ADON.
Through Storm & Sunshine. Illustrated by M. E. Edwards, A. T. H. Paterson, and the Author. Crown 8vo. Cloth, price 7s. 6d.

A. J. R.
Told at Twilight; Stories in Verse, Songs, &c. Fcap. 8vo. Cloth, price 3s. 6d.

A. K. H. B.
A Scotch Communion Sunday, to which are added Certain Discourses from a University City. By the Author of "The Recreations of a Country Parson." Second Edition. Crown 8vo. Cloth, price 5s.

ALBERT (Mary).
Holland and her Heroes to the year 1585. An Adaptation from "Motley's Rise of the Dutch Republic." Small crown 8vo. Cloth, price, 4s. 6d.

ALLEN (Rev. R.), M.A.
Abraham; his Life, Times, and Travels, 3,800 years ago. Second Edition. With Map. Post 8vo. Cloth, price 6s.

ALLEN (Grant), B.A.
Physiological Æsthetics. Large post 8vo. 9s.

AMOS (Prof. Sheldon).
Science of Law. Third Edition. Crown 8vo. Cloth, price 5s.
Volume X. of The International Scientific Series.

ANDERSON (Rev. C.), M.A.
New Readings of Old Parables. Demy 8vo. Cloth, price 4s. 6d.

Church Thought and Church Work. Edited by. Second Edition. Demy 8vo. Cloth, price 7s. 6d.

The Curate of Shyre. Second Edition. 8vo. Cloth, price 7s. 6d.

ANDERSON (Col. R. P.).
Victories and Defeats. An Attempt to explain the Causes which have led to them. An Officer's Manual. Demy 8vo. Cloth, price 14s.

ANDERSON (R. C.), C.E.
Tables for Facilitating the Calculation of every Detail in connection with Earthen and Masonry Dams. Royal 8vo. Cloth, price £2 2s.

ANSON (Lieut.-Col. The Hon. A.), V.C., M.P.
The Abolition of Purchase and the Army Regulation Bill of 1871. Crown 8vo. Sewed, price 1s.
Army Reserves and Militia Reforms. Crown 8vo. Sewed, price 1s.
Story of the Supersessions. Crown 8vo. Sewed, price 6d.

ARCHER (Thomas).
About my Father's Business. Work amidst the Sick, the Sad, and the Sorrowing. Crown 8vo. Cloth, price 5s.

ARGYLE (Duke of).
Speeches on the Second Reading of the Church Patronage (Scotland) Bill in the House of Lords, June 2, 1874; and Earl of Camperdown's Amendment, June 9, 1874, placing the Election of Ministers in the hands of Ratepayers. Crown 8vo. Sewed, price 1s.

Army of the North German Confederation.
A Brief Description of its Organization, of the Different Branches of the Service and their *rôle* in War, of its Mode of Fighting, &c., &c. Translated from the Corrected Edition, by permission of the Author, by Colonel Edward Newdigate. Demy 8vo. Cloth, price 5s.

AUBERTIN (J. J.).
Camoens' Lusiads. Portuguese Text, with Translation by. With Map and Portraits. 2 vols. Demy 8vo. Price 30s.

Aunt Mary's Bran Pie.
By the author of "St. Olave's." Illustrated. Cloth, price 3s. 6d.

Aurora.
A Volume of Verse. Fcap. 8vo. Cloth, price 5s.

BAGEHOT (Walter).
Some Articles on the Depreciation of Silver, and Topics connected with it. Demy 8vo. Price 5s.

BAGEHOT (Walter)—*continued*.
Physics and Politics; or, Thoughts on the Application of the Principles of "Natural Selection" and "Inheritance" to Political Society. Fourth Edition. Crown 8vo. Cloth, price 4s.
Volume II. of The International Scientific Series.
The English Constitution. A New Edition, Revised and Corrected, with an Introductory Dissertation on Recent Changes and Events. Crown 8vo. Cloth, price 7s. 6d.
Lombard Street. A Description of the Money Market. Seventh Edition. Crown 8vo. Cloth, price 7s. 6d.

BAGOT (Alan).
Accidents in Mines: their Causes and Prevention. Crown 8vo. Cloth, price 6s.

BAIN (Alexander), LL.D.
Mind and Body: the Theories of their relation. Fifth Edition. Crown 8vo. Cloth, price 4s.
Volume IV. of The International Scientific Series.

BAKER (Sir Sherston, Bart.).
Halleck's International Law; or Rules Regulating the Intercourse of States in Peace and War. A New Edition, revised, with Notes and Cases. 2 vols. Demy 8vo. Cloth, price 38s.

BALDWIN (Capt. J. H.), F.Z.S.
The Large and Small Game of Bengal and the North-Western Provinces of India. 4to. With numerous Illustrations. Second Edition. Cloth, price 21s.

BANKS (Mrs. G. L.).
God's Providence House. New Edition. Crown 8vo. Cloth, price 3s. 6d.

BARING (T. C.), M.A., M.P.
Pindar in English Rhyme. Being an Attempt to render the Epinikian Odes with the principal remaining Fragments of Pindar into English Rhymed Verse. Small Quarto. Cloth, price 7s.

BARLEE (Ellen).
Locked Out: a Tale of the Strike. With a Frontispiece. Royal 16mo. Cloth, price 1s. 6d.

BARNES (William).
An Outline of English Speechcraft. Crown 8vo. Cloth, price 4s.

BARTLEY (George C. T.).
Domestic Economy: Thrift in Every Day Life. Taught in Dialogues suitable for Children of all ages. Small crown 8vo. Cloth, limp, 2s.

BAUR (Ferdinand), Dr. Ph.
A Philological Introduction to Greek and Latin for Students. Translated and adapted from the German of. By C. KEGAN PAUL, M.A. Oxon., and the Rev. E. D. STONE, M.A., late Fellow of King's College, Cambridge, and Assistant Master at Eton. Crown 8vo. Cloth, price 6s.

BAYNES (Rev. Canon R. H.)
At the Communion Time. A Manual for Holy Communion. With a preface by the Right Rev. the Lord Bishop of Derry and Raphoe. Cloth, price 1s. 6d.
*** Can also be had bound in French morocco, price 2s. 6d.; Persian morocco, price 3s.; Calf, or Turkey morocco, price 3s. 6d.

Home Songs for Quiet Hours. Fourth and cheaper Edition. Fcap. 8vo. Cloth, price 2s. 6d.
This may also be had handsomely bound in morocco with gilt edges.

BECKER (Bernard H.).
The Scientific Societies of London. Crown 8vo. Cloth, price 5s.

BELLINGHAM (Henry), Barrister-at-Law.
Social Aspects of Catholicism and Protestantism in their Civil Bearing upon Nations. Translated and adapted from the French of M. le Baron de Haulleville. With a Preface by His Eminence Cardinal Manning. Crown 8vo. Cloth, price 6s.

BENNETT (Dr. W. C.).
Narrative Poems & Ballads. Fcap. 8vo. Sewed in Coloured Wrapper, price 1s.

BENNETT (Dr. W. C.)—*continued.*
Songs for Sailors. Dedicated by Special Request to H. R. H. the Duke of Edinburgh. With Steel Portrait and Illustrations. Crown 8vo. Cloth, price 3s. 6d.
An Edition in Illustrated Paper Covers, price 1s.
Songs of a Song Writer. Crown 8vo. Cloth, price 6s.

BENNIE (Rev. J. N.), M.A.
The Eternal Life. Sermons preached during the last twelve years. Crown 8vo. Cloth, price 6s.

BERNARD (Bayle).
Samuel Lover, the Life and Unpublished Works of. In 2 vols. With a Steel Portrait. Post 8vo. Cloth, price 21s.

BERNSTEIN (Prof.).
The Five Senses of Man. With 91 Illustrations. Second Edition. Crown 8vo. Cloth, price 5s.
Volume XXI. of The International Scientific Series.

BETHAM - EDWARDS (Miss M.).
Kitty. With a Frontispiece. Crown 8vo. Cloth, price 6s.

BISCOE (A. C.).
The Earls of Middleton, Lords of Clermont and of Fettercairn, and the Middleton Family. Crown 8vo. Cloth, price 10s. 6d.

BISSET (A.)
History of the Struggle for Parliamentary Government in England. 2 vols. Demy 8vo. Cloth, price 24s.

BLASERNA (Prof. Pietro).
The Theory of Sound in its Relation to Music. With numerous Illustrations. Crown 8vo. Cloth, price 5s.
Volume XXII. of The International Scientific Series.

Blue Roses; or, Helen Malinofska's Marriage. By the Author of "Véra." 2 vols. Fifth Edition. Cloth, gilt tops, 12s.
*** Also a Cheaper Edition in 1 vol. With frontispiece. Crown 8vo. Cloth, price 6s.

BLUME (Major W.).

The Operations of the German Armies in France, from Sedan to the end of the war of 1870-71. With Map. From the Journals of the Head-quarters Staff. Translated by the late E. M. Jones, Maj. 20th Foot, Prof. of Mil. Hist., Sandhurst. Demy 8vo. Cloth, price 9s.

BOGUSLAWSKI (Capt. A. von).

Tactical Deductions from the War of 1870-71. Translated by Colonel Sir Lumley Graham, Bart., late 18th (Royal Irish) Regiment. Third Edition, Revised and Corrected. Demy 8vo. Cloth, price 7s.

BONWICK (J.), F.R.G.S.

Egyptian Belief and Modern Thought. Large post 8vo. Cloth, price 10s. 6d.

Pyramid Facts and Fancies. Crown 8vo. Cloth, price 5s.

The Tasmanian Lily. With Frontispiece. Crown 8vo. Cloth, price 5s.

Mike Howe, the Bushranger of Van Diemen's Land. With Frontispiece. Crown 8vo. Cloth, price 5s.

BOSWELL (R. B.), M.A., Oxon.

Metrical Translations from the Greek and Latin Poets, and other Poems. Crown 8vo. Cloth, price 5s.

BOWEN (H. C.), M. A.

Studies in English, for the use of Modern Schools. Small Crown 8vo. Cloth, price 1s. 6d.

BOWRING (L.), C.S.I.

Eastern Experiences. Illustrated with Maps and Diagrams. Demy 8vo. Cloth, price 16s.

BOWRING (Sir John).

Autobiographical Recollections. With Memoir by Lewin B. Bowring. Demy 8vo. Price 14s.

BRADLEY (F. H.).

Ethical Studies. Critical Essays in Moral Philosophy. Large post 8vo. Cloth, price 9s.

BRADLEY (F. H.)—continued.

Mr. Sidgwick's Hedonism: an Examination of the Main Argument of "The Methods of Ethics." Demy 8vo., sewed, price 2s. 6d.

Brave Men's Footsteps. By the Editor of "Men who have Risen." A Book of Example and Anecdote for Young People. With Four Illustrations by C. Doyle. Third Edition. Crown 8vo. Cloth, price 3s. 6d.

BRIALMONT (Col. A.).

Hasty Intrenchments. Translated by Lieut. Charles A. Empson, R.A. With Nine Plates. Demy 8vo. Cloth, price 6s.

BROOKE (Rev. J. M. S.), M. A.

Heart, be Still. A Sermon preached in Holy Trinity Church, Southall. Imperial 32mo. Sewed, price 6d.

BROOKE (Rev. S. A.), M.A.

The Late Rev. F. W. Robertson, M.A., Life and Letters of. Edited by.

I. Uniform with the Sermons. 2 vols. With Steel Portrait. Price 7s. 6d.

II. Library Edition. 8vo. With Two Steel Portraits. Price 12s.

III. A Popular Edition, in 1 vol. 8vo. Price 6s.

Theology in the English Poets. — COWPER, COLERIDGE, WORDSWORTH, and BURNS. Third Edition. Post 8vo. Cloth, price 9s.

Christ in Modern Life. Eleventh Edition. Crown 8vo. Cloth, price 7s. 6d.

Sermons. First Series. Ninth Edition. Crown 8vo. Cloth, price 6s.

Sermons. Second Series. Third Edition Crown 8vo. Cloth, price 7s.

The Fight of Faith. Sermons preached on various occasions. Third Edition. Crown 8vo. Cloth, price 7s. 6d.

Frederick Denison Maurice: The Life and Work of. A Memorial Sermon. Crown 8vo. Sewed, price 1s.

BROOKE (W. G.), M.A.
The Public Worship Regulation Act. With a Classified Statement of its Provisions, Notes, and Index. Third Edition, revised and corrected. Crown 8vo. Cloth, price 3s. 6d.
Six Privy Council Judgments—1850-1872. Annotated by. Third Edition. Crown 8vo. Cloth, price 9s.

BROUN (J. A.).
Magnetic Observations at Trevandrum and Augustia Malley. Vol. I. 4to. Cloth, price 63s.
The Report from above, separately sewed, price 21s.

BROWN (Rev. J. Baldwin), B.A.
The Higher Life. Its Reality, Experience, and Destiny. Fourth Edition. Crown 8vo. Cloth, price 7s. 6d.
Doctrine of Annihilation in the Light of the Gospel of Love. Five Discourses. Third Edition. Crown 8vo. Cloth, price 2s. 6d.

BROWN (J. Croumbie), LL.D.
Reboisement in France; or, Records of the Replanting of the Alps, the Cevennes, and the Pyrenees with Trees, Herbage, and Bush. Demy 8vo. Cloth, price 12s. 6d.
The Hydrology of Southern Africa. Demy 8vo. Cloth, price 10s. 6d.

BRYANT (W. C.)
Poems. Red-line Edition. With 24 Illustrations and Portrait of the Author. Crown 8vo. Cloth extra, price 7s. 6d.
A Cheaper Edition, with Frontispiece. Small crown 8vo. Cloth, price 3s. 6d.

BUCHANAN (Robert).
Poetical Works. Collected Edition, in 3 vols., with Portrait. Crown 8vo. Cloth, price 6s. each.
Master-Spirits. Post 8vo. Cloth, price 10s. 6d.

BULKELEY (Rev. H. J.).
Walled in, and other Poems. Crown 8vo. Cloth, price 5s.

BURCKHARDT (Jacob).
The Civilization of the Period of the Renaissance in Italy. Authorized translation, by S. G. C. Middlemore. 2 vols. Demy 8vo. Cloth, price 24s.

BURTON (Mrs. Richard).
The Inner Life of Syria, Palestine, and the Holy Land. With Maps, Photographs, and Coloured Plates. 2 vols. Second Edition. Demy 8vo. Cloth, price 24s.

BURTON (Capt. Richard F.).
The Gold Mines of Midian and the Ruined Midianite Cities. A Fortnight's Tour in North Western Arabia. With numerous Illustrations. Second Edition. Demy 8vo. Cloth, price 18s.

CALDERON.
Calderon's Dramas: The Wonder-Working Magician—Life is a Dream—The Purgatory of St. Patrick. Translated by Denis Florence MacCarthy. Post 8vo. Cloth, price 10s.

CARLISLE (A. D.), B. A.
Round the World in 1870. A Volume of Travels, with Maps. New and Cheaper Edition. Demy 8vo. Cloth, price 6s.

CARNE (Miss E. T.).
The Realm of Truth. Crown 8vo. Cloth, price 5s. 6d.

CARPENTER (E.).
Narcissus and other Poems. Fcap. 8vo. Cloth, price 5s.

CARPENTER (W. B.), LL.D., M.D., F.R.S., &c.
The Principles of Mental Physiology. With their Applications to the Training and Discipline of the Mind, and the Study of its Morbid Conditions. Illustrated. Fourth Edition. 8vo. Cloth, price 12s.

CAVALRY OFFICER.
Notes on Cavalry Tactics, Organization, &c. With Diagrams. Demy 8vo. Cloth, price 12s.

CHAPMAN (Hon. Mrs. E. W.).
A Constant Heart. A Story.
2 vols. Cloth, gilt tops, price 12s.

Children's Toys, and some Elementary Lessons in General Knowledge which they teach. Illustrated. Crown 8vo. Cloth, price 5s.

CHRISTOPHERSON (The late Rev. Henry), M.A.
Sermons. With an Introduction by John Rae, LL.D., F.S.A. Second Series. Crown 8vo. Cloth, price 6s.

CLERK (Mrs. Godfrey).
'Ilâm en Nâs. Historical Tales and Anecdotes of the Times of the Early Khalifahs. Translated from the Arabic Originals. Illustrated with Historical and Explanatory Notes. Crown 8vo. Cloth, price 7s.

CLERY (C.), Capt.
Minor Tactics. With 26 Maps and Plans. Third and revised Edition. Demy 8vo. Cloth, price 16s.

CLODD (Edward), F.R.A.S.
The Childhood of the World: a Simple Account of Man in Early Times. Third Edition. Crown 8vo. Cloth, price 3s.
A Special Edition for Schools. Price 1s.

The Childhood of Religions. Including a Simple Account of the Birth and Growth of Myths and Legends. Third Thousand. Crown 8vo. Cloth, price 5s.
A Special Edition for Schools. Price 1s. 6d.

COLERIDGE (Sara).
Pretty Lessons in Verse for Good Children, with some Lessons in Latin, in Easy Rhyme. A New Edition. Illustrated. Fcap. 8vo. Cloth, price 3s. 6d.

Phantasmion. A Fairy Tale. With an Introductory Preface by the Right Hon. Lord Coleridge, of Ottery St. Mary. A New Edition. Illustrated. Crown 8vo. Cloth, price 7s. 6d.

COLERIDGE (Sara)—*continued*.
Memoir and Letters of Sara Coleridge. Edited by her Daughter. With Index. 2 vols. With Two Portraits. Third Edition, Revised and Corrected. Crown 8vo. Cloth, price 24s.
Cheap Edition. With one Portrait. Cloth, price 7s. 6d.

COLLINS (Mortimer).
Inn of Strange Meetings, and other Poems. Crown 8vo. Cloth, price 5s.

COLLINS (Rev. R.), M.A.
Missionary Enterprise in the East. With special reference to the Syrian Christians of Malabar, and the results of modern Missions. With Four Illustrations. Crown 8vo. Cloth, price 6s.

CONGREVE (Richard), M.A., M.R.C.P.L.
Human Catholicism. Two Sermons delivered at the Positivist School on the Festival of Humanity, 87 and 88, January 1, 1875 and 1876. Demy 8vo. Sewed, price 1s.

Religion of Humanity; the Annual Address delivered at the Positivist School, 19, Chapel-street, Lamb's Conduit-street, W.C., on the Festival of Humanity, January 1, 1878.

COOKE (M. C.), M.A., LL.D.
Fungi; their Nature, Influences, Uses, &c. Edited by the Rev. M. J. Berkeley, M.A., F.L.S. With Illustrations. Second Edition. Crown 8vo. Cloth, price 5s.
Volume XIV. of The International Scientific Series.

COOKE (Prof. J. P.)
The New Chemistry. With 31 Illustrations. Third Edition. Crown 8vo. Cloth, price 5s.
Volume IX. of The International Scientific Series.

Scientific Culture. Crown 8vo. Cloth, price 1s.

COOPER (T. T.), F.R.G.S.
The Mishmee Hills: an Account of a Journey made in an Attempt to Penetrate Thibet from Assam, to open New Routes for Commerce. Second Edition. With Four Illustrations and Map. Post 8vo. Cloth, price 10s. 6d.

Cornhill Library of Fiction (The). Crown 8vo. Cloth, price 3s. 6d. per volume.
Half-a-Dozen Daughters. By J. Masterman.
The House of Raby. By Mrs. G. Hooper.
A Fight for Life. By Moy Thomas.
Robin Gray. By Charles Gibbon.
One of Two; or, A Left-Handed Bride. By J. Hain Friswell.
God's Providence House. By Mrs. G. L. Banks.
For Lack of Gold. By Charles Gibbon.
Abel Drake's Wife. By John Saunders.
Hirell. By John Saunders.

CORY (Lieut. Col. Arthur).
The Eastern Menace; or, Shadows of Coming Events. Crown 8vo. Cloth, price 5s.
Ione. A Poem in Four Parts. Fcap. 8vo. Cloth, price 5s.

Cosmos.
A Poem. Fcap. 8vo. Cloth, price 3s. 6d.

COX (Rev. Sir G. W.), Bart.
A History of Greece from the Earliest Period to the end of the Persian War. 2 vols. Demy 8vo. Cloth, price 36s.
The Mythology of the Aryan Nations. 2 vols. Demy 8vo. Cloth, price 28s.
A General History of Greece from the Earliest Period to the Death of Alexander the Great, with a sketch of the subsequent History to the present time. Crown 8vo. Cloth, price 7s. 6d.
Tales of Ancient Greece. Third Edition. Small Crown 8vo. Cloth, price 6s.
School History of Greece. With Maps. Fcap. 8vo. Cloth, price 3s. 6d.
The Great Persian War from the Histories of Herodotus. New Edition. Fcap. 8vo. Cloth, price 3s. 6d.
A Manual of Mythology in the form of Question and Answer. Third Edition. Fcap. 8vo. Cloth, price 3s.

COX (Rev. Samuel).
Salvator Mundi; or, Is Christ the Saviour of all Men? Fifth Edition. Crown 8vo. Cloth, price 5s.

CRESSWELL (Mrs. G.).
The King's Banner. Drama in Four Acts. Five Illustrations. 4to. Cloth, price 10s. 6d.

CROMPTON (Henry).
Industrial Conciliation. Fcap. 8vo. Cloth, price 2s. 6d.

CUMMINS (H. I.), M.A.
Parochial Charities of the City of London. Sewed, price 1s.

CURWEN (Henry).
Sorrow and Song: Studies of Literary Struggle. Henry Mürger—Novalis—Alexander Petőfi—Honoré de Balzac—Edgar Allan Poe—André Chénier. 2 vols. Crown 8vo. Cloth, price 15s.

DANCE (Rev. C. D.).
Recollections of Four Years in Venezuela. With Three Illustrations and a Map. Crown 8vo. Cloth, price 7s. 6d.

D'ANVERS (N. R.).
The Suez Canal: Letters and Documents descriptive of its Rise and Progress in 1854-56. By Ferdinand de Lesseps. Translated by. Demy 8vo. Cloth, price 10s. 6d.
Little Minnie's Troubles. An Every-day Chronicle. With Four Illustrations by W. H. Hughes. Fcap. Cloth, price 3s. 6d.
Pixie's Adventures; or, the Tale of a Terrier. With 21 Illustrations. 16mo. Cloth, price 4s. 6d.

DAVIDSON (Rev. Samuel), D.D., LL.D.
The New Testament, translated from the Latest Greek Text of Tischendorf. A new and thoroughly revised Edition. Post 8vo. Cloth, price 10s. 6d.
Canon of the Bible; Its Formation, History, and Fluctuations. Second Edition. Small crown 8vo. Cloth, price 5s.

DAVIES (G. Christopher).
Mountain, Meadow, and Mere: a Series of Outdoor Sketches of Sport, Scenery, Adventures, and Natural History. With Sixteen Illustrations by Bosworth W. Harcourt. Crown 8vo. Cloth, price 6s.

Rambles and Adventures of Our School Field Club. With Four Illustrations. Crown 8vo. Cloth, price 5s.

DAVIES (Rev. J. L.), M.A.
Theology and Morality. Essays on Questions of Belief and Practice. Crown 8vo. Cloth, price 7s. 6d.

DAWSON (George), M.A.
Prayers, with a Discourse on Prayer. Edited by his Wife. Fifth Edition. Crown 8vo. Price 6s.

Sermons on Disputed Points and Special Occasions. Edited by his Wife. Second Edition. Crown 8vo. Cloth, price 6s.

Sermons on Daily Life and Duty. Edited by his Wife. Second Edition. Crown 8vo. Cloth, price 6s.

DE L'HOSTE (Col. E. P.).
The Desert Pastor, Jean Jarousseau. Translated from the French of Eugène Pelletan. With a Frontispiece. New Edition. Fcap. 8vo. Cloth, price 3s. 6d.

DE REDCLIFFE (Viscount Stratford), P.C., K.G., G.C.B.
Why am I a Christian? Fifth Edition. Crown 8vo. Cloth, price 3s.

DE TOCQUEVILLE (A.).
Correspondence and Conversations of, with Nassau William Senior, from 1834 to 1859. Edited by M. C. M. Simpson. 2 vols. Post 8vo. Cloth, price 21s.

DE VERE (Aubrey).
Alexander the Great. A Dramatic Poem. Small crown 8vo. Cloth, price 5s.

The Infant Bridal, and Other Poems. A New and Enlarged Edition. Fcap. 8vo. Cloth, price 7s. 6d.

DE VERE (Aubrey).—continued.
The Legends of St. Patrick, and Other Poems. Small crown 8vo. Cloth, price 5s.

St. Thomas of Canterbury. A Dramatic Poem. Large fcap. 8vo. Cloth, price 5s.

Antar and Zara: an Eastern Romance. INISFAIL, and other Poems, Meditative and Lyrical. Fcap. 8vo. Price 6s.

The Fall of Rora, the Search after Proserpine, and other Poems, Meditative and Lyrical. Fcap. 8vo. Price 6s.

DENNIS (J.).
English Sonnets. Collected and Arranged. Elegantly bound. Fcap. 8vo. Cloth, price 3s. 6d.

DOBSON (Austin).
Vignettes in Rhyme and Vers de Société. Third Edition. Fcap. 8vo. Cloth, price 5s.

Proverbs in Porcelain. By the Author of "Vignettes in Rhyme." Second Edition. Crown 8vo. 6s.

DOWDEN (Edward), LL.D.
Shakspere: a Critical Study of his Mind and Art. Third Edition. Large Post 8vo. Cloth, price 12s.

Studies in Literature, 1789-1877. Large Post 8vo. Cloth, price 12s.

Poems. Second Edition. Fcap. 8vo. Cloth, price 5s.

DOWNTON (Rev. H.), M.A.
Hymns and Verses. Original and Translated. Small crown 8vo. Cloth, price 3s. 6d.

DRAPER (J W.), M.D., LL.D.
History of the Conflict between Religion and Science. Eleventh Edition. Crown 8vo. Cloth, price 5s.
Volume XIII. of The International Scientific Series.

DREW (Rev. G. S.), M.A.
Scripture Lands in connection with their History. Second Edition. 8vo. Cloth, price 10s. 6d.
Nazareth: Its Life and Lessons. Third Edition. Crown 8vo. Cloth, price 5s.
The Divine Kingdom on Earth as it is in Heaven. 8vo. Cloth, price 10s. 6d.
The Son of Man: His Life and Ministry. Crown 8vo. Cloth, price 7s. 6d.

DREWRY (G. O.), M.D.
The Common-Sense Management of the Stomach. Fourth Edition. Fcap. 8vo. Cloth, price 2s. 6d.

DREWRY (G. O.), M.D., and BARTLETT (H. C.), Ph.D., F.C.S.
Cup and Platter: or, Notes on Food and its Effects. Small 8vo. Cloth, price 2s. 6d.

DRUMMOND (Miss).
Tripps Buildings. A Study from Life, with Frontispiece. Small crown 8vo. Cloth, price 3s. 6d.

DURAND (Lady).
Imitations from the German of Spitta and Terstegen. Fcap. 8vo. Cloth, price 4s.

DU VERNOIS (Col. von Verdy).
Studies in leading Troops. An authorized and accurate Translation by Lieutenant H. J. T. Hildyard, 71st Foot. Parts I. and II. Demy 8vo. Cloth, price 7s.

EDEN (Frederick).
The Nile without a Dragoman. Second Edition. Crown 8vo. Cloth, price 7s. 6d.

EDMONDS (Herbert).
Well Spent Lives: a Series of Modern Biographies. Crown 8vo. Price 5s.

EDWARDS (Rev. Basil).
Minor Chords; Or, Songs for the Suffering: a Volume of Verse. Fcap. 8vo. Cloth, price 3s. 6d.; paper, price 2s. 6d.

ELLIOT (Lady Charlotte).
Medusa and other Poems. Crown 8vo. Cloth, price 6s.

ELLIOTT (Ebenezer), The Corn Law Rhymer.
Poems. Edited by his son, the Rev. Edwin Elliott, of St. John's, Antigua. 2 vols. Crown 8vo. Cloth, price 18s.

ELSDALE (Henry).
Studies in Tennyson's Idylls. Crown 8vo. Cloth, price 5s.

ENGLISH CLERGYMAN.
An Essay on the Rule of Faith and Creed of Athanasius. Shall the Rubric preceding the Creed be removed from the Prayerbook? Sewed. 8vo. Price 1s.

Epic of Hades (The).
By a New Writer. Author of "Songs of Two Worlds." Fourth and finally revised Edition. Fcap. 8vo. Cloth, price 7s. 6d.

Eros Agonistes.
Poems. By E. B. D. Fcap. 8vo. Cloth, price 3s. 6d.

Essays on the Endowment of Research.
By Various Writers.
LIST OF CONTRIBUTORS.
Mark Pattison, B. D.
James S. Cotton, B. A.
Charles E. Appleton, D. C. L.
Archibald H. Sayce, M. A.
Henry Clifton Sorby, F. R. S.
Thomas K. Cheyne, M. A.
W. T. Thiselton Dyer, M. A.
Henry Nettleship, M. A.
Square crown octavo. Cloth, price 10s. 6d.

EVANS (Mark).
The Gospel of Home Life. Crown 8vo. Cloth, price 4s. 6d.
The Story of our Father's Love, told to Children; being a New and Enlarged Edition of Theology for Children. With Four Illustrations. Fcap. 8vo. Cloth, price 3s. 6d.
A Book of Common Prayer and Worship for Household Use, compiled exclusively from the Holy Scriptures. Fcap. 8vo. Cloth, price 2s. 6d.

C. Kegan Paul & Co.'s Publications. 11

EX-CIVILIAN.
Life in the Mofussil: or, Civilian Life in Lower Bengal. 2 vols. Large post 8vo. Price 14s.

EYRE (Maj.-Gen. Sir V.), C.B., K.C.S.I., &c.
Lays of a Knight-Errant in many Lands. Square crown 8vo. With Six Illustrations. Cloth, price 7s. 6d.

FARQUHARSON (M.).
I. Elsie Dinsmore. Crown 8vo. Cloth, price 3s. 6d.
II. Elsie's Girlhood. Crown 8vo. Cloth, price 3s. 6d.
III. Elsie's Holidays at Roselands. Crown 8vo. Cloth, price 3s. 6d.

FERRIS (Henry Weybridge).
Poems. Fcap. 8vo. Cloth, price 5s.

Folkestone Ritual Case (The). The Argument, Proceedings Judgment, and Report, revised by the several Counsel engaged. Demy 8vo. Cloth, price 25s.

FOOTMAN (Rev. H.), M.A.
From Home and Back; or, Some Aspects of Sin as seen in the Light of the Parable of the Prodigal. Crown 8vo. Cloth, price 5s.

FOWLE (Rev. Edmund).
Latin Primer Rules made Easy. Crown 8vo. Cloth, price 3s.

FOWLE (Rev. T. W.), M.A.
The Reconciliation of Religion and Science. Being Essays on Immortality, Inspiration, Miracles, and the Being of Christ. Demy 8vo. Cloth, price 10s. 6d.

FOX-BOURNE (H. R.).
The Life of John Locke, 1632—1704. 2 vols. Demy 8vo. Cloth, price 28s.

FRASER (Donald).
Exchange Tables of Sterling and Indian Rupee Currency, upon a new and extended system, embracing Values from One Farthing to One Hundred Thousand Pounds, and at Rates progressing, in Sixteenths of a Penny, from 1s. 9d. to 2s. 3d. per Rupee. Royal 8vo. Cloth, price 10s. 6d.

FRISWELL (J. Hain).
The Better Self. Essays for Home Life. Crown 8vo. Cloth, price 6s.

One of Two; or, A Left-Handed Bride. With a Frontispiece. Crown 8vo. Cloth, price 3s. 6d.

FYTCHE (Lieut.-Gen. Albert), C.S.I., late Chief Commissioner of British Burma.
Burma Past and Present, with Personal Reminiscences of the Country. With Steel Portraits, Chromolithographs, Engravings on Wood, and Map. 2 vols. Demy 8vo. Cloth, price 30s.

GAMBIER (Capt. J. W.), R.N.
Servia. Crown 8vo. Cloth, price 5s.

GARDNER (H.).
Sunflowers. A Book of Verses. Fcap. 8vo. Cloth, price 5s.

GARDNER (J.), M.D.
Longevity: The Means of Prolonging Life after Middle Age. Fourth Edition, revised and enlarged. Small crown 8vo. Cloth, price 4s.

GARRETT (E.).
By Still Waters. A Story for Quiet Hours. With Seven Illustrations. Crown 8vo. Cloth, price 6s.

G. H. T.
Verses, mostly written in India. Crown 8vo. Cloth, price 6s.

GIBBON (Charles).
For Lack of Gold. With a Frontispiece. Crown 8vo. Illustrated Boards, price 2s.

Robin Gray. With a Frontispiece. Crown 8vo. Illustrated boards, price 2s.

GILBERT (Mrs.).
Autobiography and other Memorials. Edited by Josiah Gilbert. Third Edition. With Portrait and several Wood Engravings. Crown 8vo. Cloth, price 7s. 6d.

GILL (Rev. W. W.), B.A.
Myths and Songs from the South Pacific. With a Preface by F. Max Müller, M.A., Professor of Comparative Philology at Oxford. Post 8vo. Cloth, price 9s.

GODKIN (James).
The Religious History of Ireland: Primitive, Papal, and Protestant. Including the Evangelical Missions, Catholic Agitations, and Church Progress of the last half Century. 8vo. Cloth, price 12s.

GOETZE (Capt. A. von).
Operations of the German Engineers during the War of 1870-1871. Published by Authority, and in accordance with Official Documents. Translated from the German by Colonel G. Graham, V.C., C.B., R.E. With 6 large Maps. Demy 8vo. Cloth, price 21s.

GODWIN (William).
William Godwin: His Friends and Contemporaries. With Portraits and Facsimiles of the handwriting of Godwin and his Wife. By C. Kegan Paul. 2 vols. Demy 8vo. Cloth, price 28s.

The Genius of Christianity Unveiled. Being Essays never before published. Edited, with a Preface, by C. Kegan Paul. Crown 8vo. Cloth, price 7s. 6d.

GOLDIE (Lieut. M. H. G.)
Hebe: a Tale. Fcap. 8vo. Cloth, price 5s.

GOODENOUGH (Commodore J. G.), R.N., C.B., C.M.G.
Memoir of, with Extracts from his Letters and Journals. Edited by his Widow. With Steel Engraved Portrait. Square 8vo. Cloth, 5s.
*** Also a Library Edition with Maps, Woodcuts, and Steel Engraved Portrait. Square post 8vo Cloth, price 14s.

GOODMAN (W.).
Cuba, the Pearl of the Antilles. Crown 8vo. Cloth, price 7s. 6d.

GOULD (Rev. S. Baring), M.A.
The Vicar of Morwenstow: a Memoir of the Rev. R. S. Hawker. With Portrait. Third Edition, revised. Square post 8vo. Cloth, 10s. 6d.

GRANVILLE (A. B.), M.D., F.R.S., &c.
Autobiography of A. B. Granville, F.R.S., etc. Edited, with a brief account of the concluding years of his life, by his youngest Daughter, Paulina B. Granville. 2 vols. With a Portrait. Second Edition. Demy 8vo. Cloth, price 32s.

GREY (John), of Dilston.
John Grey (of Dilston): Memoirs. By Josephine E. Butler. New and Revised Edition. Crown 8vo. Cloth, price 3s. 6d.

GRIFFITH (Rev. T.), A.M.
Studies of the Divine Master. Demy 8vo. Cloth, price 12s.

GRIFFITHS (Capt. Arthur).
Memorials of Millbank, and Chapters in Prison History. With Illustrations by R. Goff and the Author. 2 vols. Post 8vo. Cloth, price 21s.

GRIMLEY (Rev. H. N.), M.A., Professor of Mathematics in the University College of Wales.
Tremadoc Sermons, chiefly on the SPIRITUAL BODY, the UNSEEN WORLD, and the DIVINE HUMANITY. Second Edition. Crown 8vo. Cloth, price 6s.

GRÜNER (M. L.).
Studies of Blast Furnace Phenomena. Translated by L. D. B. Gordon, F.R.S.E.; F.G.S. Demy 8vo. Cloth, price 7s. 6d.

GURNEY (Rev. Archer).
Words of Faith and Cheer. A Mission of Instruction and Suggestion. Crown 8vo. Cloth, price 6s.

First Principles in Church and State. Demy 8vo. Sewed, price 1s. 6d.

HAECKEL (Prof. Ernst).

The History of Creation. Translation revised by Professor E. Ray Lankester, M.A., F.R.S. With Coloured Plates and Genealogical Trees of the various groups of both plants and animals. 2 vols. Second Edition. Post 8vo. Cloth, price 32s.

The History of the Evolution of Man. With numerous Illustrations. 2 vols. Post 8vo.

HAKE (A. Egmont).

Paris Originals, with twenty etchings, by Léon Richeton. Large post 8vo. Cloth, price 14s.

Halleck's International Law or Rules. Regulating the Intercourse of States in Peace and War. A New Edition, revised, with Notes and Cases. 2 vols. Demy 8vo. Cloth, price 38s.

HARCOURT (Capt. A. F. P.).

The Shakespeare Argosy. Containing much of the wealth of Shakespeare's Wisdom and Wit, alphabetically arranged and classified. Crown 8vo. Cloth, price 6s.

HARDY (Thomas).

A Pair of Blue Eyes. New Edition. Crown 8vo. Cloth, price 6s.

HARRISON (Lieut.-Col. R.).

The Officer's Memorandum Book for Peace and War. Second Edition. Oblong 32mo. roan, elastic band and pencil, price 3s. 6d.; russia, 5s.

HAWEIS (Rev. H. R.), M.A.

Current Coin. Materialism—The Devil—Crime—Drunkenness—Pauperism—Emotion—Recreation—The Sabbath. Third Edition. Crown 8vo. Cloth, price 6s.

Speech in Season. Fourth Edition. Crown 8vo. Cloth, price 9s.

Thoughts for the Times. Tenth Edition. Crown 8vo. Cloth, price 7s. 6d.

HAWEIS (Rev. H. R.)—continued.

Unsectarian Family Prayers, for Morning and Evening for a Week, with short selected passages from the Bible. Second Edition. Square crown 8vo. Cloth, price 3s. 6d.

HAYMAN (H.), D.D., late Head Master of Rugby School.

Rugby School Sermons. With an Introductory Essay on the Indwelling of the Holy Spirit. Crown 8vo. Cloth, price 7s. 6d.

HELLWALD (Baron F. von).

The Russians in Central Asia. A Critical Examination, down to the present time, of the Geography and History of Central Asia. Translated by Lieut.-Col. Theodore Wirgman, LL.B. Large post 8vo. With Map. Cloth, price 12s.

HELVIG (Major H.).

The Operations of the Bavarian Army Corps. Translated by Captain G. S. Schwabe. With Five large Maps. In 2 vols. Demy 8vo. Cloth, price 24s.

Tactical Examples: Vol. I. The Battalion, price 15s. Vol. II. The Regiment and Brigade, price 10s. 6d. Translated from the German by Col. Sir Lumley Graham. With numerous Diagrams. Demy 8vo. Cloth.

HERFORD (Brooke).

The Story of Religion in England. A Book for Young Folk. Crown 8vo. Cloth, price 5s.

HEWLETT (Henry G.).

A Sheaf of Verse. Fcap. 8vo. Cloth, price 3s. 6d.

HINTON (James).

Life and Letters of. Edited by Ellice Hopkins, with an Introduction by Sir W. W. Gull, Bart., and Portrait engraved on Steel by C. H. Jeens. Crown 8vo. Cloth, 8s. 6d.

The Place of the Physician. To which is added ESSAYS ON THE LAW OF HUMAN LIFE, AND ON THE RELATION BETWEEN ORGANIC AND INORGANIC WORLDS. Second Edition. Crown 8vo. Cloth, price 3s. 6d.

HINTON (James).—*continued.*
Physiology for Practical Use. By various Writers. With 50 Illustrations. 2 vols. Second Edition. Crown 8vo. Cloth, price 12s. 6d.

An Atlas of Diseases of the Membrana Tympani. With Descriptive Text. Post 8vo. Price £6 6s.

The Questions of Aural Surgery. With Illustrations. 2 vols. Post 8vo. Cloth, price 12s. 6d.

H. J. C.
The Art of Furnishing. A Popular Treatise on the Principles of Furnishing, based on the Laws of Common Sense, Requirement, and Picturesque Effect. Small crown 8vo. Cloth, price 3s. 6d.

HOCKLEY (W. B.).
Tales of the Zenana; or, A Nuwab's Leisure Hours. By the Author of "Pandurang Hari." With a Preface by Lord Stanley of Alderley. 2 vols. Crown 8vo. Cloth, price 21s.

Pandurang Hari; or, Memoirs of a Hindoo. A Tale of Mahratta Life sixty years ago. With a Preface by Sir H. Bartle E. Frere, G.C.S.I., &c. Crown 8vo. Cloth, price 6s.

HOFFBAUER (Capt.).
The German Artillery in the Battles near Metz. Based on the official reports of the German Artillery. Translated by Capt. E. O. Hollist. With Map and Plans. Demy 8vo. Cloth, price 21s.

HOLMES (E. G. A.).
Poems. Fcap. 8vo. Cloth, price 5s.

HOLROYD (Major W. R. M.).
Tas-hil ul Kālām; or, Hindustani made Easy. Crown 8vo. Cloth, price 5s.

HOOPER (Mary).
Little Dinners: How to Serve them with Elegance and Economy. Thirteenth Edition. Crown 8vo. Cloth, price 5s.

HOOPER (Mary).—*continued.*
Cookery for Invalids, Persons of Delicate Digestion, and Children. Crown 8vo. Cloth, price 3s. 6d.

Every-Day Meals. Being Economical and Wholesome Recipes for Breakfast, Luncheon, and Supper. Second Edition. Crown 8vo. Cloth, price 5s.

HOOPER (Mrs. G.).
The House of Raby. With a Frontispiece. Crown 8vo. Cloth, price 3s. 6d.

HOPKINS (Ellice).
Life and Letters of James Hinton, with an Introduction by Sir W. W. Gull, Bart., and Portrait engraved on Steel by C. H. Jeens. Crown 8vo. Cloth, price 8s. 6d.

HOPKINS (M.).
The Port of Refuge; or, Counsel and Aid to Shipmasters in Difficulty, Doubt, or Distress. Crown 8vo. Second and Revised Edition. Cloth, price 6s.

HORNE (William), M.A.
Reason and Revelation: an Examination into the Nature and Contents of Scripture Revelation, as compared with other Forms of Truth. Demy 8vo. Cloth, price 12s.

HORNER (The Misses).
Walks in Florence. A New and thoroughly Revised Edition. 2 vols. crown 8vo. Cloth limp. With Illustrations.
 Vol. I.—Churches, Streets, and Palaces. 10s. 6d. Vol. II.—Public Galleries and Museums. 5s.

HOWARD (Mary M.).
Beatrice Aylmer, and other Tales. Crown 8vo. Cloth, price 6s.

HOWARD (Rev. G. B.).
An Old Legend of St. Paul's. Fcap. 8vo. Cloth, price 4s. 6d.

HOWELL (James).
A Tale of the Sea, Sonnets, and other Poems. Fcap. 8vo. Cloth, price 5s.

HUGHES (Allison).
Penelope and other Poems. Fcap. 8vo. Cloth, price 4s. 6d.

HULL (Edmund C. P.).
The European in India.
With a MEDICAL GUIDE FOR ANGLO-INDIANS. By R. R. S. Mair, M.D., F.R.C.S.E. Third Edition, Revised and Corrected. Post 8vo. Cloth, price 6s.

HUMPHREY (Rev. W.).
Mr. Fitzjames Stephen and Cardinal Bellarmine. Demy 8vo. Sewed, price 1s.

IGNOTUS.
Culmshire Folk. A Novel. New and Cheaper Edition. Crown 8vo. Cloth, price 6s.

INCHBOLD (J. W.).
Annus Amoris. Sonnets. Foolscap 8vo. Cloth, price 4s. 6d.

INGELOW (Jean).
The Little Wonder-horn. A Second Series of "Stories Told to a Child." With Fifteen Illustrations. Small 8vo. Cloth, price 2s. 6d.

Indian Bishoprics. By an Indian Churchman. Demy 8vo. 6d.

International Scientific Series (The).
I. The Forms of Water in Clouds and Rivers, Ice and Glaciers. By J. Tyndall, LL.D., F.R.S. With 25 Illustrations. Seventh Edition. Crown 8vo. Cloth, price 5s.

II. Physics and Politics; or, Thoughts on the Application of the Principles of "Natural Selection" and "Inheritance" to Political Society. By Walter Bagehot. Fourth Edition. Crown 8vo. Cloth, price 4s.

III. Foods. By Edward Smith, M.D., LL.B., F.R.S. With numerous Illustrations. Fifth Edition. Crown 8vo. Cloth, price 5s.

IV. Mind and Body: The Theories of their Relation. By Alexander Bain, LL.D. With Four Illustrations. Fifth Edition. Crown 8vo. Cloth, price 4s.

V. The Study of Sociology. By Herbert Spencer. Sixth Edition. Crown 8vo. Cloth, price 5s.

International Scientific Series (The)—*continued*.
VI. On the Conservation of Energy. By Balfour Stewart, M.A., LL.D., F.R.S. With 14 Illustrations. Fourth Edition. Crown 8vo. Cloth, price 5s.

VII. Animal Locomotion; or, Walking, Swimming, and Flying. By J. B. Pettigrew, M.D., F.R.S., etc. With 130 Illustrations. Second Edition. Crown 8vo. Cloth, price 5s.

VIII. Responsibility in Mental Disease. By Henry Maudsley, M.D. Third Edition. Crown 8vo. Cloth, price 5s.

IX. The New Chemistry. By Professor J. P. Cooke, of the Harvard University. With 31 Illustrations. Fourth Edition. Crown 8vo. Cloth, price 5s.

X. The Science of Law. By Professor Sheldon Amos. Third Edition. Crown 8vo. Cloth, price 5s.

XI. Animal Mechanism. A Treatise on Terrestrial and Aerial Locomotion. By Professor E. J. Marey. With 117 Illustrations. Second Edition. Crown 8vo. Cloth, price 5s.

XII. The Doctrine of Descent and Darwinism. By Professor Oscar Schmidt (Strasburg University). With 26 Illustrations. Third Edition. Crown 8vo. Cloth, price 5s.

XIII. The History of the Conflict between Religion and Science. By J. W. Draper, M.D., LL.D. Eleventh Edition. Crown 8vo. Cloth, price 5s.

XIV. Fungi; their Nature, Influences, Uses, &c. By M. C. Cooke, M.A., LL.D. Edited by the Rev. M. J. Berkeley, M.A., F.L.S. With numerous Illustrations. Second Edition. Crown 8vo. Cloth, price 5s.

XV. The Chemical Effects of Light and Photography. By Dr. Hermann Vogel (Polytechnic Academy of Berlin). With 100 Illustrations. Third and Revised Edition. Crown 8vo. Cloth, price 5s.

International Scientific Series (The)—*continued*.

XVI. **The Life and Growth of Language.** By William Dwight Whitney, Professor of Sanskrit and Comparative Philology in Yale College, New Haven. Second Edition. Crown 8vo. Cloth, price

XVII. **Money and the Mechanism of Exchange.** By W. Stanley Jevons, M.A., F.R.S. Third Edition. Crown 8vo. Cloth, price 5s.

XVIII. **The Nature of Light:** With a General Account of Physical Optics. By Dr. Eugene Lommel, Professor of Physics in the University of Erlangen. With 188 Illustrations and a table of Spectra in Chromo-lithography. Second Edition. Crown 8vo. Cloth, price 5s.

XIX. **Animal Parasites and Messmates.** By Monsieur Van Beneden, Professor of the University of Louvain, Correspondent of the Institute of France. With 83 Illustrations. Second Edition. Crown 8vo. Cloth, price 5s.

XX. **Fermentation.** By Professor Schützenberger, Director of the Chemical Laboratory at the Sorbonne. With 28 Illustrations. Second Edition. Crown 8vo. Cloth, price 5s.

XXI. **The Five Senses of Man.** By Professor Bernstein, of the University of Halle. With 91 Illustrations. Second Edition. Crown 8vo. Cloth, price 5s.

XXII. **The Theory of Sound in its Relation to Music.** By Professor Pietro Blaserna, of the Royal University of Rome. With numerous Illustrations. Second Edition. Crown 8vo. Cloth, price 5s.

XXIII. **Studies in Spectrum Analysis.** By J. Norman Lockyer, F.R.S. With six photographic Illustrations of Spectra, and numerous engravings on wood. Crown 8vo. Second Edition. Cloth, price 6s. 6d.

Forthcoming Volumes.

Prof. W. KINGDON CLIFFORD, M.A. The First Principles of the Exact Sciences explained to the Non-mathematical.

International Scientific Series (The).

Forthcoming Vols.—continued.

W. B. CARPENTER, LL.D., F.R.S. The Physical Geography of the Sea.

Sir JOHN LUBBOCK, Bart., F.R.S. On Ants and Bees.

Prof. W. T. THISELTON DYER, B.A., B.Sc. Form and Habit in Flowering Plants.

Prof. MICHAEL FOSTER, M.D. Protoplasm and the Cell Theory.

H. CHARLTON BASTIAN, M.D., F.R.S. The Brain as an Organ of Mind.

Prof. A. C. RAMSAY, LL.D., F.R.S. Earth Sculpture: Hills, Valleys, Mountains, Plains, Rivers, Lakes; how they were Produced, and how they have been Destroyed.

P. BERT (Professor of Physiology, Paris). Forms of Life and other Cosmical Conditions.

Prof. T. H. HUXLEY. The Crayfish: an Introduction to the Study of Zoology.

The Rev. A SECCHI, D.J., late Director of the Observatory at Rome. The Stars.

Prof. J. ROSENTHAL, of the University of Erlangen. General Physiology of Muscles and Nerves.

Prof. A. DE QUATREFAGES, Membre de l'Institut. The Human Race.

Prof. THURSTON. The Steam Engine. With numerous Engravings.

FRANCIS GALTON, F.R.S. Psychometry.

J. W. JUDD, F.R.S. The Laws of Volcanic Action.

Prof. F. N. BALFOUR. The Embryonic Phases of Animal Life.

J. LUYS, Physician to the Hospice de la Salpétrière. The Brain and its Functions. With Illustrations.

Dr. CARL SEMPER. Animals and their Conditions of Existence.

Prof. WURTZ. Atoms and the Atomic Theory.

C. Kegan Paul & Co.'s Publications.

International Scientific Series (The).
Forthcoming Vols.—continued.

GEORGE J. ROMANES, F.L.S. Animal Intelligence.

ALFRED W. BENNETT. A Handbook of Cryptogamic Botany.

JACKSON (T. G.).
Modern Gothic Architecture. Crown 8vo. Cloth, price 5s.

JACOB (Maj.-Gen. Sir G. Le Grand), K.C.S.I., C.B.
Western India Before and during the Mutinies. Pictures drawn from life. Second Edition. Crown 8vo. Cloth, price 7s. 6d.

JENKINS (E.) and RAYMOND (J.), Esqs.
A Legal Handbook for Architects, Builders, and Building Owners. Second Edition Revised. Crown 8vo. Cloth, price 6s.

JENKINS (Rev. R. C.), M.A.
The Privilege of Peter and the Claims of the Roman Church confronted with the Scriptures, the Councils, and the Testimony of the Popes themselves. Fcap. 8vo. Cloth, price 3s. 6d.

JENNINGS (Mrs. Vaughan).
Rahel: Her Life and Letters. With a Portrait from the Painting by Daffinger. Square post 8vo. Cloth, price 7s. 6d.

JEVONS (W. Stanley), M.A., F.R.S.
Money and the Mechanism of Exchange. Second Edition. Crown 8vo. Cloth, price 5s.
Volume XVII. of The International Scientific Series.

JONES (Lucy).
Puddings and Sweets. Being Three Hundred and Sixty-Five Receipts approved by Experience. Crown 8vo., price 2s. 6d.

KAUFMANN (Rev. M.), B.A.
Socialism: Its Nature, its Dangers, and its Remedies considered. Crown 8vo. Cloth, price 7s. 6d.

KER (David).
The Boy Slave in Bokhara. A Tale of Central Asia. With Illustrations. Crown 8vo. Cloth, price 5s.

The Wild Horseman of the Pampas. Illustrated. Crown 8vo. Cloth, price 5s.

KING (Alice).
A Cluster of Lives. Crown 8vo. Cloth, price 7s. 6d.

KING (Mrs. Hamilton).
The Disciples. A Poem. Third Edition, with some Notes. Crown 8vo. Cloth, price 7s. 6d.

Aspromonte, and other Poems. Second Edition. Fcap. 8vo. Cloth, price 4s. 6d.

KINGSLEY (Charles), M.A.
Letters and Memories of his Life. Edited by his WIFE. With 2 Steel engraved Portraits and numerous Illustrations on Wood, and a Facsimile of his Handwriting. Eleventh Edition. 2 vols., demy 8vo. Cloth, price 36s.

All Saints' Day and other Sermons. Second Edition. Crown 8vo. Cloth, price 7s. 6d.

Letters to Young Men on Betting and Gambling. 8vo. sewed, price 7s. 6d. per 100.

KNIGHT (A. F. C.).
Poems. Fcap 8vo. Cloth, price 5s.

LACORDAIRE (Rev. Père).
Life: Conferences delivered at Toulouse. A New and Cheaper Edition. Crown 8vo. Cloth, price 3s. 6d.

Lady of Lipari (The).
A Poem in Three Cantos. Fcap. 8vo. Cloth, price 5s.

LAMBERT (Cowley), F.R.G.S.
A Trip to Cashmere and Ladâk. With numerous Illustrations. Crown 8vo. Cloth, price 7s. 6d.

LAURIE (J. S.).
Educational Course of Secular School Books for India:
The First Hindustani Reader. Stiff linen wrapper, price 6d.
The Second Hindustani Reader. Stiff linen wrapper, price 6d.
The Oriental (English) Reader. Book I., price 6d.; II., price 7½d.; III., price 9d.; IV., price 1s.
Geography of India; with Maps and Historical Appendix, tracing the Growth of the British Empire in Hindustan. Fcap. 8vo. Cloth, price 1s. 6d.

LAYMANN (Capt.).
The Frontal Attack of Infantry. Translated by Colonel Edward Newdigate. Crown 8vo. Cloth, price 2s. 6d.

L. D. S.
Letters from China and Japan. With Illustrated Title-page. Crown 8vo. Cloth, price 7s. 6d.

LEANDER (Richard).
Fantastic Stories. Translated from the German by Paulina B. Granville. With Eight full-page Illustrations by M. E. Fraser-Tytler. Crown 8vo. Cloth, price 5s.

LEE (Rev. F. G.), D.C.L.
The Other World; or, Glimpses of the Supernatural. 2 vols. A New Edition. Crown 8vo. Cloth, price 15s.

LEE (Holme).
Her Title of Honour. A Book for Girls. New Edition. With a Frontispiece. Crown 8vo. Cloth, price 5s.

LENOIR (J.).
Fayoum; or, Artists in Egypt. A Tour with M. Gérome and others. With 13 Illustrations. A New and Cheaper Edition. Crown 8vo. Cloth, price 3s. 6d.

LEWIS (Mary A.).
A Rat with Three Tales. With Four Illustrations by Catherine F. Frere. Cloth, price 5s.

LOCKER (F.).
London Lyrics. A New and Revised Edition, with Additions and a Portrait of the Author. Crown 8vo. Cloth, elegant, price 6s.
Also, an Edition for the People. Fcap. 8vo. Cloth, price 2s. 6d.

LOCKYER (J. Norman), F.R.S.
Studies in Spectrum Analysis; with six photographic illustrations of Spectra, and numerous engravings on wood. Second Edition. Crown 8vo. Cloth, price 6s. 6d.
Vol. XXIII. of the International Scientific Series.

LOMMEL (Dr. E.).
The Nature of Light: With a General Account of Physical Optics. Second Edition. With 188 Illustrations and a Table of Spectra in Chromo-lithography. Second Edition. Crown 8vo. Cloth, price 5s.
Volume XVIII. of The International Scientific Series.

LORIMER (Peter), D.D.
John Knox and the Church of England: His Work in her Pulpit, and his Influence upon her Liturgy, Articles, and Parties. Demy 8vo. Cloth, price 12s.

John Wiclif and his English Precursors, by Gerhard Victor Lechler. Translated from the German, with additional Notes. 2 vols. Demy 8vo. Cloth, price 21s.

LOTHIAN (Roxburghe).
Dante and Beatrice from 1282 to 1290. A Romance. 2 vols. Post 8vo. Cloth, price 24s.

LOVER (Samuel), R.H.A.
The Life of Samuel Lover, R.H.A.; Artistic, Literary, and Musical. With Selections from his Unpublished Papers and Correspondence. By Bayle Bernard. 2 vols. With a Portrait. Post 8vo. Cloth, price 21s.

LUCAS (Alice).
Translations from the Works of German Poets of the 18th and 19th Centuries. Fcap. 8vo. Cloth, price 5s.

C. Kegan Paul & Co.'s Publications.

LYONS (R. T.), Surg.-Maj. Bengal Army.
A Treatise on Relapsing Fever. Post 8vo. Cloth, price 7s. 6d.

MACAULAY (J.), M.A., M.D., Edin.
The Truth about Ireland: Tours of Observation in 1872 and 1875. With Remarks on Irish Public Questions. Being a Second Edition of "Ireland in 1872," with a New and Supplementary Preface. Crown 8vo. Cloth, price 3s. 6d.

MAC CLINTOCK (L.).
Sir Spangle and the Dingy Hen. Illustrated. Square crown 8vo., price 2s. 6d.

MAC DONALD (G.).
Malcolm. With Portrait of the Author engraved on Steel. Fourth Edition. Crown 8vo. Price 6s.
The Marquis of Lossie. Second Edition. Crown 8vo. Cloth, price 6s.
St. George and St. Michael. Crown 8vo. Cloth, 6s.

MAC KENNA (S. J.).
Plucky Fellows. A Book for Boys. With Six Illustrations. Second Edition. Crown 8vo. Cloth, price 3s. 6d.
At School with an Old Dragoon. With Six Illustrations. Second Edition. Crown 8vo. Cloth, price 5s.

MACLACHLAN (A. N. C.), M.A.
William Augustus, Duke of Cumberland: being a Sketch of his Military Life and Character, chiefly as exhibited in the General Orders of His Royal Highness, 1745—1747. With Illustrations. Post 8vo. Cloth, price 15s.

MACNAUGHT (Rev. John).
Cœna Domini: An Essay on the Lord's Supper, its Primitive Institution, Apostolic Uses, and Subsequent History. Demy 8vo. Cloth, price 14s.

MAGNUSSON (Eirikr), M.A., and PALMER (E.H.), M.A.
Johan Ludvig Runeberg's Lyrical Songs, Idylls and Epigrams. Fcap. 8vo. Cloth, price 5s.

MAIR (R. S.), M.D., F.R.C.S.E.
The Medical Guide for Anglo-Indians. Being a Compendium of Advice to Europeans in India, relating to the Preservation and Regulation of Health. With a Supplement on the Management of Children in India. Second Edition. Crown 8vo. Limp cloth, price 3s. 6d.

MALDEN (H. E. and E. E.)
Princes and Princesses. Illustrated. Small crown 8vo. Cloth, price 2s. 6d.

MANNING (His Eminence Cardinal).
Essays on Religion and Literature. By various Writers. Third Series. Demy 8vo. Cloth, price 10s. 6d.
The Independence of the Holy See, with an Appendix containing the Papal Allocution and a translation. Cr. 8vo. Cloth, price 5s.
The True Story of the Vatican Council. Crown 8vo. Cloth, price 5s.

MAREY (E. J.).
Animal Mechanics. A Treatise on Terrestrial and Aerial Locomotion. With 117 Illustrations. Second Edition. Crown 8vo. Cloth, price 5s.
Volume XI. of The International Scientific Series.

MARRIOTT (Maj.-Gen. W. F.), C.S.I.
A Grammar of Political Economy. Crown 8vo. Cloth, price 6s.

MASTERMAN (J.).
Worth Waiting for. A New Novel. 3 vols. Crown 8vo. Cloth.
Half-a-dozen Daughters. With a Frontispiece. Crown 8vo. Cloth, price 3s. 6d.

MAUDSLEY (Dr. H.).
Responsibility in Mental Disease. Second Edition. Crown 8vo. Cloth, price 5s.
Volume VIII. of The International Scientific Series.

MAUGHAN (W. C.).
The Alps of Arabia; or, Travels through Egypt, Sinai, Arabia, and the Holy Land. With Map. Second Edition. Demy 8vo. Cloth, price 5s.

MAURICE (C. E.).
Lives of English Popular Leaders. No. 1.—STEPHEN LANGTON. Crown 8vo. Cloth, price 7s. 6d. No. 2.—TYLER, BALL, and OLDCASTLE. Crown 8vo. Cloth, price 7s. 6d.

Mazzini (Joseph).
A Memoir. By E. A. V. Two Photographic Portraits. Second Edition. Crown 8vo. Cloth, price 5s.

MEDLEY (Lieut.-Col. J. G.), R.E.
An Autumn Tour in the United States and Canada. Crown 8vo. Cloth, price 5s.

MEREDITH (George).
The Ordeal of Richard Feverel. A History of Father and Son. In one vol. with Frontispiece. Crown 8vo. Cloth, price 6s.

MICKLETHWAITE (J. T.), F.S.A.
Modern Parish Churches: Their Plan, Design, and Furniture. Crown 8vo. Cloth, price 7s. 6d.

MIDDLETON (The Lady).
Ballads. Square 16mo. Cloth, price 3s. 6d.

MILLER (Edward).
The History and Doctrines of Irvingism; or, the so-called Catholic and Apostolic Church. 2 vols. Large post 8vo. Cloth, price 25s.

MILLER (Robert).
The Romance of Love. Fcap. 8vo. Cloth, price 5s.

MILNE (James).
Tables of Exchange for the Conversion of Sterling Money into Indian and Ceylon Currency, at Rates from 1s. 8d. to 2s. 3d. per Rupee. Second Edition. Demy 8vo. Cloth, price £2 2s.

MIVART (St. George), F.R.S.
Contemporary Evolution: An Essay on some recent Social Changes. Post 8vo. Cloth, price 7s. 6d.

MOCKLER (E.).
A Grammar of the Baloochee Language, as it is spoken in Makran (Ancient Gedrosia), in the Persia-Arabic and Roman characters. Fcap. 8vo. Cloth, price 5s.

MOFFAT (Robert Scott).
The Economy of Consumption; an Omitted Chapter in Political Economy, with special reference to the Questions of Commercial Crises and the Policy of Trades Unions; and with Reviews of the Theories of Adam Smith, Ricardo, J. S. Mill, Fawcett, &c. Demy 8vo. Cloth, price 18s.

The Principles of a Time Policy: being an Exposition of a Method of Settling Disputes between Employers and Labourers in regard to Time and Wages, by a simple Process of Mercantile Barter, without recourse to Strikes or Locks-out. Reprinted from "The Economy of Consumption," with a Preface and Appendix containing Observations on some Reviews of that book, and a Re-criticism of the Theories of Ricardo and J. S. Mill on Rent, Value, and Cost of Production. Demy 8vo. Cloth, price 3s. 6d.

MOLTKE (Field-Marshal Von).
Letters from Russia. Translated by Robina Napier. Crown 8vo. Cloth, price 6s.

MOORE (Rev. D.), M.A.
Christ and His Church. By the Author of "The Age and the Gospel," &c. Crown 8vo. Cloth, price 3s. 6d.

MORE (R. Jasper).
Under the Balkans. Notes of a Visit to the District of Philippopolis in 1876. With a Map and Illustrations from Photographs. Crown 8vo. Cloth, price 6s.

MORELL (J. R.).
Euclid Simplified in Method and Language. Being a Manual of Geometry. Compiled from the most important French Works, approved by the University of Paris and the Minister of Public Instruction. Fcap. 8vo. Cloth, price 2s. 6d.

MORICE (Rev. F. D.), M.A.
The Olympian and Pythian Odes of Pindar. A New Translation in English Verse. Crown 8vo. Cloth, price 7s. 6d.

MORLEY (Susan).
Aileen Ferrers. A Novel. 2 vols. Crown 8vo. Cloth.

Throstlethwaite. A Novel. 3 vols. Crown 8vo. Cloth.

MORLEY (Susan)—*continued.*
Margaret Chetwynd. A Novel. 3 vols. Crown 8vo. Cloth.

MORSE (E. S.), Ph.D.
First Book of Zoology. With numerous Illustrations. Crown 8vo. Cloth; price 5s.

MORSHEAD (E. D. A.)
The Agamemnon of Æschylus. Translated into English verse. With an Introductory Essay. Crown 8vo. Cloth, price 5s.

MOSTYN (Sydney).
Perplexity. A Novel. 3 vols. Crown 8vo. Cloth.

MUSGRAVE (Anthony).
Studies in Political Economy. Crown 8vo. Cloth, price 6s.

My Sister Rosalind. A Novel. By the Author of "Christiana North," and "Under the Limes." 2 vols. Cloth.

NAAKÉ (J. T.).
Slavonic Fairy Tales. From Russian, Servian, Polish, and Bohemian Sources. With Four Illustrations. Crown 8vo. Cloth, price 5s.

NEWMAN (J. H.), D.D.
Characteristics from the Writings of. Being Selections from his various Works. Arranged with the Author's personal approval. Third Edition. With Portrait. Crown 8vo. Cloth, price 6s.
** A Portrait of the Rev. Dr. J. H. Newman, mounted for framing, can be had, price 2s. 6d.

NEW WRITER (A).
Songs of Two Worlds. Third Edition. Complete in one volume with Portrait. Fcap. 8vo. Cloth, price 7s. 6d.

The Epic of Hades. Fourth and finally revised Edition. Fcap. 8vo. Cloth, price 7s. 6d.

NICHOLAS (Thomas), Ph. D., F.G.S.
The Pedigree of the English People: an Argument, Historical and Scientific, on the Formation and Growth of the Nation, tracing Race-admixture in Britain from the earliest times, with especial reference to the incorporation of the Celtic Aborigines. Fifth edition. Demy 8vo. Cloth, price 16s.

NICHOLSON (Edward B.), Librarian of the London Institution.
The Christ Child, and other Poems. Crown 8vo. Cloth, price 4s. 6d.

NOAKE (Major R. Compton).
The Bivouac; or, Martial Lyrist, with an Appendix—Advice to the Soldier. Fcap. 8vo. Price 5s. 6d.

NOBLE (J. A.).
The Pelican Papers. Reminiscences and Remains of a Dweller in the Wilderness. Crown 8vo. Cloth, price 6s.

NORMAN PEOPLE (The).
The Norman People, and their Existing Descendants in the British Dominions and the United States of America. Demy 8vo. Cloth, price 21s.

NORRIS (Rev. Alfred).
The Inner and Outer Life Poems. Fcap. 8vo. Cloth, price 6s.

Northern Question (The); Or, Russia's Policy in Turkey unmasked. Demy 8vo. Sewed, price 1s.

Notes on Cavalry Tactics, Organization, &c. By a Cavalry Officer. With Diagrams. Demy 8vo. Cloth, price 12s.

NOTREGE (John), A.M.
The Spiritual Function of a Presbyter in the Church of England. Crown 8vo. Cloth, red edges, price 3s. 6d.

Oriental Sporting Magazine (The). A Reprint of the first 5 Volumes, in 2 Volumes. Demy 8vo. Cloth, price 28s.

Our Increasing Military Difficulty, and one Way of Meeting it. Demy 8vo. Stitched, price 1s.

PAGE (Capt. S. F.).
Discipline and Drill. Cheaper Edition. Crown 8vo. Price 1s.

PALGRAVE, (W. Gifford).
Hermann Agha; An Eastern Narrative. Third and Cheaper Edition. Crown 8vo. Cloth, price 6s.

PANDURANG HARI;
Or, Memoirs of a Hindoo.
With an Introductory Preface by Sir H. Bartle E. Frere, G.C.S.I., C.B. Crown 8vo. Price 6s.

PARKER (Joseph), D.D.
The Paraclete: An Essay on the Personality and Ministry of the Holy Ghost, with some reference to current discussions/ Second Edition. Demy 8vo. Cloth, price 12s.

PARR (Harriet).
Echoes of a Famous Year.
Crown 8vo. Cloth, price 8s. 6d.

PAUL (C. Kegan).
Goethe's Faust. A New Translation in Rime. Crown 8vo. Cloth, price 6s.

William Godwin: His Friends and Contemporaries. With Portraits and Facsimiles of the Handwriting of Godwin and his Wife. 2 vols. Square post 8vo. Cloth, price 28s.

The Genius of Christianity Unveiled. Being Essays by William Godwin never before published. Edited, with a Preface, by C. Kegan Paul. Crown 8vo. Cloth price 7s. 6d.

PAUL (Margaret Agnes).
Gentle and Simple: A Story.
2 vols. Crown 8vo. Cloth, gilt tops, price 12s.

PAYNE (John).
Songs of Life and Death.
Crown 8vo Cloth, price 5s.

PAYNE (Prof. J. F.).
Lectures on Education.
Price 6d. each.
II. Fröbel and the Kindergarten System. Second Edition.

A Visit to German Schools: Elementary Schools in Germany. Notes of a Professional Tour to inspect some of the Kindergartens, Primary Schools, Public Girls Schools, and Schools for Technical Instruction in Hamburgh, Berlin, Dresden, Weimar, Gotha, Eisenach, in the autumn of 1874. With Critical Discussions of the General Principles and Practice of Kindergartens and other Schemes of Elementary Education. Crown 8vo. Cloth, price 4s. 6d.

PEACOCKE (Georgiana).
Rays from the Southern Cross: Poems. Crown 8vo. With Sixteen Full-page Illustrations by the Rev. P. Walsh. Cloth elegant, price 10s. 6d.

PELLETAN (E.).
The Desert Pastor, Jean Jarousseau. Translated from the French. By Colonel E. P. De L'Hoste. With a Frontispiece. New Edition. Fcap. 8vo. Cloth, price 3s. 6d.

PENNELL (H. Cholmondeley).
Pegasus Resaddled. By the Author of "Puck on Pegasus," &c. &c. With Ten Full-page Illustrations by George Du Maurier. Second Edition. Fcap. 4to. Cloth elegant, price 12s. 6d.

PENRICE (Maj. J.), B.A.
A Dictionary and Glossary of the Ko-ran. With copious Grammatical References and Explanations of the Text. 4to. Cloth, price 21s.

PERCIVAL (Rev. P.).
Tamil Proverbs, with their English Translation. Containing upwards of Six Thousand Proverbs. Third Edition. Demy 8vo. Sewed, price 9s.

PESCHEL (Dr. Oscar).
The Races of Man and their Geographical Distribution. Large crown 8vo. Cloth, price 9s.

PETTIGREW (J. Bell), M.D., F.R.S.
Animal Locomotion; or, Walking, Swimming, and Flying. With 130 Illustrations. Second Edition. Crown 8vo. Cloth, price 5s.
Volume VII. of The International Scientific Series.

PFEIFFER (Emily).
Glan Alarch: His Silence and Song. A Poem. Crown 8vo. price 6s.

Gerard's Monument and Other Poems. Second Edition. Crown 8vo. Cloth, price 6s.

Poems. Crown 8vo. Cloth, price 6s.

PIGGOT (J.), F.S.A., F.R.G.S.
Persia—Ancient and Modern. Post 8vo. Cloth, price 10s. 6d.

PLAYFAIR (Lieut.-Col.), Her Britannic Majesty's Consul-General in Algiers.
Travels in the Footsteps of Bruce in Algeria and Tunis. Illustrated by facsimiles of Bruce's original Drawings, Photographs, Maps, &c. Royal 4to. Cloth, bevelled boards, gilt leaves, price £3 3s.

POOR (Henry V.).
Money and its Laws, embracing a History of Monetary Theories and a History of the Currencies of the United States. Demy 8vo. Cloth, price 21s.

POUSHKIN (A. S.).
Russian Romance. Translated from the Tales of Belkin, etc. By Mrs. J. Buchan Telfer (*née* Mouravieff*).* Crown 8vo. Cloth, price 7s. 6d.

POWER (H.).
Our Invalids: How shall we Employ and Amuse Them? Fcap. 8vo. Cloth, price 2s. 6d.

POWLETT (Lieut. N.), R.A.
Eastern Legends and Stories in English Verse. Crown 8vo. Cloth, price 5s.

PRESBYTER.
Unfoldings of Christian Hope. An Essay showing that the Doctrine contained in the Damnatory Clauses of the Creed commonly called Athanasian is unscriptural. Small crown 8vo. Cloth, price 4s. 6d.

PRICE (Prof. Bonamy).
Currency and Banking. Crown 8vo. Cloth, price 6s.

Chapters on Practical Political Economy. Being the Substance of Lectures delivered before the University of Oxford. Large post 8vo. Cloth, price 12s.

PROCTOR (Richard A.), B.A.
Our Place among Infinities. A Series of Essays contrasting our little abode in space and time with the Infinities around us. To which are added Essays on "Astrology," and "The Jewish Sabbath." Third Edition. Crown 8vo. Cloth, price 6s.

The Expanse of Heaven. A Series of Essays on the Wonders of the Firmament. With a Frontispiece. Third Edition. Crown 8vo. Cloth, price 6s.

Proteus and Amadeus. A Correspondence. Edited by Aubrey De Vere. Crown 8vo. Cloth, price 5s.

PUBLIC SCHOOLBOY.
The Volunteer, the Militiaman, and the Regular Soldier. Crown 8vo. Cloth, price 5s.

Punjaub (The) and North Western Frontier of India. By an old Punjauber. Crown 8vo. Cloth, price 5s.

RAM (James).
The Philosophy of War. Small Crown 8vo. Cloth, price 3s. 6d.

READ (Carveth).
On the Theory of Logic: An Essay. Crown 8vo. Cloth, price 6s.

REANEY (Mrs. G. S.).
Blessing and Blessed; a Sketch of Girl Life. With a frontispiece. Crown 8vo. Cloth, price 5s.

Waking and Working; or, from Girlhood to Womanhood. With a Frontispiece. Crown 8vo. Cloth, price 5s.

Sunshine Jenny and other Stories. Three Illustrations. Royal 16mo. Cloth, price 1s. 6d.

Sunbeam Willie, and other Stories. Three Illustrations. Royal 16mo. Cloth, price 1s. 6d.

RHOADES (James).
Timoleon. A Dramatic Poem. Fcap. 8vo. Cloth, price 5s.

RIBOT (Prof. Th.).
English Psychology. Second Edition. A Revised and Corrected Translation from the latest French Edition. Large post 8vo. Cloth, price 9s.

RIBOT (Prof. Th.)—*continued.*
Heredity: A Psychological Study on its Phenomena, its Laws, its Causes, and its Consequences. Large crown 8vo. Cloth, price 9s.

RINK (Chevalier Dr. Henry).
Greenland: Its People and its Products. By the Chevalier Dr. HENRY RINK, President of the Greenland Board of Trade. With sixteen Illustrations, drawn by the Eskimo, and a Map. Edited by Dr. ROBERT BROWN. Crown 8vo. Price 10s. 6d.

ROBERTSON (The Late Rev. F. W.), M.A., of Brighton.
Notes on Genesis. Third Edition. Crown 8vo., price 5s.

New and Cheaper Editions:—
The Late Rev. F. W. Robertson, M.A., Life and Letters of. Edited by the Rev. Stopford Brooke, M.A., Chaplain in Ordinary to the Queen.
I. 2 vols., uniform with the Sermons. With Steel Portrait. Crown 8vo. Cloth, price 7s. 6d.
II. Library Edition, in Demy 8vo., with Two Steel Portraits. Cloth price 12s.
III. A Popular Edition, in 1 vol. Crown 8vo. Cloth, price 6s.

Sermons. Four Series. Small crown 8vo. Cloth, price 3s. 6d. each.

Expository Lectures on St. Paul's Epistles to the Corinthians. A New Edition. Small crown 8vo. Cloth, price 5s.

Lectures and Addresses, with other literary remains. A New Edition. Crown 8vo. Cloth, price 5s.

An Analysis of Mr. Tennyson's "In Memoriam." (Dedicated by Permission to the Poet-Laureate.) Fcap. 8vo. Cloth, price 2s.

The Education of the Human Race. Translated from the German of Gotthold Ephraim Lessing. Fcap. 8vo. Cloth, price 2s. 6d.

The above Works can also be had half-bound in morocco.

** A Portrait of the late Rev. F. W. Robertson, mounted for framing, can be had, price 2s. 6d.

ROBINSON (A. Mary F.).
A Handful of Honeysuckle. Fcap. 8vo. Cloth, price 3s. 6d.

ROSS (Mrs. E.), ("Nelsie Brook").
Daddy's Pet. A Sketch from Humble Life. With Six Illustrations. Royal 16mo. Cloth, price 1s.

RUSSELL (E. R.).
Irving as Hamlet. Second Edition. Demy 8vo. Sewed, price 1s.

RUSSELL (Major Frank S.).
Russian Wars with Turkey, Past and Present. With Two Maps. Second Edition. Crown 8vo., price 6s.

RUTHERFORD (John).
The Secret History of the Fenian Conspiracy; its Origin, Objects, and Ramifications. 2 vols. Post 8vo. Cloth, price 18s.

SADLER (S. W.), R.N.
The African Cruiser. A Midshipman's Adventures on the West Coast. With Three Illustrations. Second Edition. Crown 8vo. Cloth, price 3s. 6d.

SAMAROW (G.).
For Sceptre and Crown. A Romance of the Present Time. Translated by Fanny Wormald. 2 vols. Crown 8vo. Cloth, price 15s.

SAUNDERS (Katherine).
Gideon's Rock, and other Stories. Crown 8vo. Cloth, price 6s.

Joan Merryweather, and other Stories. Crown 8vo. Cloth, price 6s.

Margaret and Elizabeth. A Story of the Sea. Crown 8vo. Cloth, price 6s.

SAUNDERS (John).
Israel Mort, Overman: a Story of the Mine. Crown 8vo. Price 6s.

Hirell. With Frontispiece. Crown 8vo. Cloth, price 3s. 6d.
Cheap Edition. With Frontispiece, price 2s.

Abel Drake's Wife. With Frontispiece. Crown 8vo. Cloth, price 3s. 6d.
Cheap Edition. With Frontispiece, price 2s.

SCHELL (Maj. von).
The Operations of the First Army under Gen. Von Goeben. Translated by Col. C. H. von Wright. Four Maps. Demy 8vo. Cloth, price 9s.

The Operations of the First Army under Gen. Von Steinmetz. Translated by Captain E. O. Hollist. Demy 8vo. Cloth, price 10s. 6d.

SCHELLENDORF, (Maj.-Gen. B. von).
The Duties of the General Staff. Translated from the German by Lieutenant Hare. Vol. I. Demy 8vo. Cloth, 10s. 6d.

SCHERFF (Maj. W. von).
Studies in the New Infantry Tactics. Parts I. and II. Translated from the German by Colonel Lumley Graham. Demy 8vo. Cloth, price 7s. 6d.

SCHMIDT (Prof. Oscar).
The Doctrine of Descent and Darwinism. With 26 Illustrations. Third Edition. Crown 8vo. Cloth, price 5s.
Volume XII. of The International Scientific Series.

SCHÜTZENBERGER (Prof. F.).
Fermentation. With Numerous Illustrations. Crown 8vo. Cloth, price 5s.
Volume XX. of The International Scientific Series.

SCOTT (Patrick).
The Dream and the Deed, and other Poems. Fcap. 8vo. Cloth, price 5s.

SCOTT (W. T.).
Antiquities of an Essex Parish; or, Pages from the History of Great Dunmow. Crown 8vo. Cloth, price 5s. Sewed, 4s.

SCOTT (Robert H.).
Weather Charts and Storm Warnings. Illustrated. Crown 8vo. Cloth, price 3s. 6d.

Seeking his Fortune, and other Stories. With Four Illustrations. Crown 8vo. Cloth, price 3s. 6d.

SENIOR (N. W.).
Alexis De Tocqueville. Correspondence and Conversations with Nassau W. Senior, from 1833 to 1859. Edited by M. C. M. Simpson. 2 vols. Large post 8vo. Cloth, price 21s.

Journals Kept in France and Italy. From 1848 to 1852. With a Sketch of the Revolution of 1848. Edited by his Daughter, M. C. M. Simpson. 2 vols. Post 8vo. Cloth, price 24s.

Seven Autumn Leaves from Fairyland. Illustrated with Nine Etchings. Square crown 8vo. Cloth, price 3s. 6d.

SEYD (Ernest), F.S.S.
The Fall in the Price of Silver. Its Causes, its Consequences, and their Possible Avoidance, with Special Reference to India. Demy 8vo. Sewed, price 2s. 6d.

SHADWELL (Maj.-Gen.), C.B.
Mountain Warfare. Illustrated by the Campaign of 1799 in Switzerland. Being a Translation of the Swiss Narrative compiled from the Works of the Archduke Charles, Jomini, and others. Also of Notes by General H. Dufour on the Campaign of the Valtelline in 1635. With Appendix, Maps, and Introductory Remarks. Demy 8vo. Cloth, price 16s.

SHAW (Flora L.).
Castle Blair: a Story of Youthful Lives. 2 vols. crown 8vo. Cloth, price 12s. Also, an edition in 1 vol. crown 8vo. 6s.

SHELLEY (Lady).
Shelley Memorials from Authentic Sources. With (now first printed) an Essay on Christianity by Percy Bysshe Shelley. With Portrait. Third Edition. Crown 8vo. Cloth, price 5s.

SHERMAN (Gen. W. T.).
Memoirs of General W. T. Sherman, Commander of the Federal Forces in the American Civil War. By Himself. 2 vols. With Map. Demy 8vo. Cloth, price 24s. *Copyright English Edition.*

SHILLITO (Rev. Joseph).
Womanhood: its Duties, Temptations, and Privileges. A Book for Young Women. Second Edition. Crown 8vo. Price 3s. 6d.

SHIPLEY (Rev. Orby), M.A.
Church Tracts, or Studies in Modern Problems. By various Writers. 2 vols. Crown 8vo. Cloth, price 5s. each.

SHUTE (Richard), M.A.
A Discourse on Truth. Large Post 8vo. Cloth, price 9s.

SMEDLEY (M. B.).
Boarding-out and Pauper Schools for Girls. Crown 8vo. Cloth, price 3s. 6d.

SMITH (Edward), M.D., LL.B., F.R.S.
Health and Disease, as Influenced by the Daily, Seasonal, and other Cyclical Changes in the Human System. A New Edition. Post 8vo. Cloth, price 7s. 6d.

Foods. Profusely Illustrated. Fourth Edition. Crown 8vo. Cloth, price 5s.
Volume III. of The International Scientific Series.

Practical Dietary for Families, Schools, and the Labouring Classes. A New Edition. Post 8vo. Cloth, price 3s. 6d.

Tubercular Consumption in its Early and Remediable Stages. Second Edition. Crown 8vo. Cloth, price 6s.

SMITH (Hubert).
Tent Life with English Gipsies in Norway. With Five full-page Engravings and Thirty-one smaller Illustrations by Whymper and others, and Map of the Country showing Routes. Third Edition. Revised and Corrected. Post 8vo. Cloth, price 21s.

Songs of Two Worlds. By the Author of "The Epic of Hades." Third Edition. Complete in one Volume, with Portrait. Fcap 8vo. Cloth, price 7s. 6d.

Songs for Music. By Four Friends. Square crown 8vo. Cloth, price 5s.
Containing songs by Reginald A. Gatty, Stephen H. Gatty, Greville J. Chester, and Juliana Ewing.

SPENCER (Herbert).
The Study of Sociology. Fifth Edition. Crown 8vo. Cloth, price 5s.
Volume V. of The International Scientific Series.

SPICER (H.).
Otho's Death Wager. A Dark Page of History Illustrated. In Five Acts. Fcap. 8vo. Cloth, price 5s.

STAPLETON (John).
The Thames: A Poem. Crown 8vo. Cloth, price 6s.

STEPHENS (Archibald John), LL.D.
The Folkestone Ritual Case. The Substance of the Argument delivered before the Judicial Committee of the Privy Council. On behalf of the Respondents. Demy 8vo. Cloth, price 6s.

STEVENSON (Robert Louis).
An Inland Voyage. With Frontispiece by Walter Crane. Crown 8vo. Cloth, price 7s. 6d.

STEVENSON (Rev. W. F.).
Hymns for the Church and Home. Selected and Edited by the Rev. W. Fleming Stevenson.
The most complete Hymn Book published.
The Hymn Book consists of Three Parts:—I. For Public Worship.—II. For Family and Private Worship.—III. For Children.
⁂ *Published in various forms and prices, the latter ranging from 8d. to 6s. Lists and full particulars will be furnished on application to the Publishers.*

STEWART (Prof. Balfour), M.A., LL.D., F.R.S.
On the Conservation of Energy. Fifth Edition. With Fourteen Engravings. Crown 8vo. Cloth, price 5s.
Volume VI. of The International Scientific Series.

STONEHEWER (Agnes).
Monacell: A Legend of North Wales. A Poem. Fcap. 8vo. Cloth, price 3s. 6d.

STRETTON (Hesba). Author of "Jessica's First Prayer."
Michael Lorio's Cross and other Stories. With Two Illustrations. Royal 16mo. Cloth, price 1s. 6d.

The Storm of Life. With Ten Illustrations. Twenty-first Thousand. Royal 16mo. Cloth, price 1s. 6d.

The Crew of the Dolphin. Illustrated. Fourteenth Thousand. Royal 16mo. Cloth, price 1s. 6d.

Cassy. Thirty-eighth Thousand. With Six Illustrations. Royal 16mo. Cloth, price 1s. 6d.

The King's Servants. Forty-third Thousand. With Eight Illustrations. Royal 16mo. Cloth, price 1s. 6d

Lost Gip. Fifty-ninth Thousand. With Six Illustrations. Royal 16mo. Cloth, price 1s. 6d.

* *Also a handsomely bound Edition, with Twelve Illustrations, price 2s. 6d.*

David Lloyd's Last Will. With Four Illustrations. Royal 16mo., price 2s. 6d.

The Wonderful Life. Thirteenth Thousand. Fcap. 8vo. Cloth, price 2s. 6d.

A Night and a Day. With Frontispiece. Twelfth Thousand. Royal 16mo. Limp cloth, price 6d.

Friends till Death. With Illustrations and Frontispiece. Twenty-fourth Thousand. Royal 16mo. Cloth, price 1s. 6d.; limp cloth, price 6d.

Two Christmas Stories. With Frontispiece. Twenty-first Thousand. Royal 16mo. Limp cloth, price 6d.

Michel Lorio's Cross, and Left Alone. With Frontispiece. Fifteenth Thousand. Royal 16mo. Limp cloth, price 6d.

STRETTON (Hesba)—*continued.*
Old Transome. With Frontispiece. Sixteenth Thousand. Royal 16mo. Limp cloth, price 6d.

* *Taken from "The King's Servants."*

The Worth of a Baby, and how Apple-Tree Court was won. With Frontispiece. Nineteenth Thousand. Royal 16mo. Limp cloth, price 6d.

STUBBS (Lieut.-Colonel F. W.)
The Regiment of Bengal Artillery. The History of its Organization, Equipment, and War Services. Compiled from Published Works, Official Records, and various Private Sources. With numerous Maps and Illustrations. Two Vols. Demy 8vo. Cloth, price 32s.

STUMM (Lieut. Hugo), German Military Attaché to the Khivan Expedition.
Russia's advance Eastward. Based on the Official Reports of. Translated by Capt. C. E. H. VINCENT. With Map. Crown 8vo. Cloth, price 6s.

SULLY (James), M.A.
Sensation and Intuition. Demy 8vo. Cloth, price 10s. 6d.

Pessimism: a History and a Criticism. Demy 8vo. Price 14s.

Sunnyland Stories. By the Author of "Aunt Mary's Bran Pie." Illustrated. Small 8vo. Cloth, price 3s. 6d.

Supernatural in Nature, The. A Verification of Scripture by Free Use of Science. Demy 8vo. Cloth, price 14s.

Sweet Silvery Sayings of Shakespeare. Crown 8vo. cloth gilt, price 7s. 6d.

SYME (David).
Outlines of an Industrial Science. Second Edition. Crown 8vo. Cloth, price 6s.

Tales of the Zenana. By the Author of "Pandurang Hari." 2 vols. Crown 8vo. Cloth, price 21s.

TAYLOR (Rev. J. W. A.), M.A.
Poems. Fcap. 8vo. Cloth, price 5s.

TAYLOR (Sir H.).
Works Complete. Author's Edition, in 5 vols. Crown 8vo. Cloth, price 6s. each.
Vols. I. to III. containing the Poetical Works, Vols. IV. and V. the Prose Works.

TAYLOR (Col. Meadows), C.S.I., M.R.I.A.
A Noble Queen : a Romance of Indian History. 3 vols. Crown 8vo. Cloth.

Seeta. 3 vols. Crown 8vo. Cloth.

The Confessions of a Thug. Crown 8vo. Cloth, price 6s.

Tara : a Mahratta Tale. Crown 8vo. Cloth, price 6s.

TELFER (J. Buchan), F.R.G.S., Commander R.N.
The Crimea and Trans-Caucasia. With numerous Illustrations and Maps. 2 vols. Medium 8vo. Second Edition. Cloth, price 36s.

TENNYSON (Alfred).
The Imperial Library Edition. Complete in 7 vols. Demy 8vo. Cloth, price £3 13s. 6d. ; in Roxburgh binding, £4 7s. 6d.

Author's Edition. Complete in 6 Volumes. Post 8vo. Cloth gilt ; or half-morocco, Roxburgh style :—

VOL. I. Early Poems, and English Idylls. Price 6s. ; Roxburgh, 7s. 6d.

VOL. II. Locksley Hall, Lucretius, and other Poems. Price 6s. ; Roxburgh, 7s. 6d.

VOL. III. The Idylls of the King (*Complete*). Price 7s. 6d.; Roxburgh, 9s.

VOL. IV. The Princess, and Maud. Price 6s.; Roxburgh, 7s. 6d.

VOL. V. Enoch Arden, and In Memoriam. Price 6s. ; Roxburgh, 7s. 6d.

TENNYSON (Alfred)—*continued*.
VOL. VI. Dramas. Price 7s. ; Roxburgh, 8s. 6d.

Cabinet Edition. 12 volumes. Each with Frontispiece. Fcap. 8vo. Cloth, price 2s. 6d. each.
CABINET EDITION. 12 vols. Complete in handsome Ornamental Case. 32s.

Pocket Volume Edition. 13 vols. In neat case, 36s. Ditto, ditto. Extra cloth gilt, in case, 42s.

The Guinea Edition of the Poetical and Dramatic Works, complete in 12 volumes, neatly bound and enclosed in box. Cloth, price 21s. French morocco, price 31s. 6d.

The Shilling Edition of the Poetical and Dramatic Works, in 12 vols., pocket size. Price 1s. each.

The Crown Edition. Complete in 1 volume, strongly bound in cloth, price 6s. Cloth, extra gilt leaves, price 7s. 6d. Roxburgh, half morocco, price 8s. 6d.

** Can also be had in a variety of other bindings.

Original Editions :

Poems. Small 8vo. Cloth, price 6s.

Maud, and other Poems. Small 8vo. Cloth, price 3s. 6d.

The Princess. Small 8vo. Cloth, price 3s. 6d.

Idylls of the King. Small 8vo. Cloth, price 5s.

Idylls of the King. Complete. Small 8vo. Cloth, price 6s.

The Holy Grail, and other Poems. Small 8vo. Cloth, price 4s. 6d.

Gareth and Lynette. Small 8vo. Cloth, price 3s.

Enoch Arden, &c. Small 8vo. Cloth, price 3s. 6d.

In Memoriam. Small 8vo. Cloth, price 4s.

TENNYSON (Alfred)—*continued.*
Queen Mary. A Drama. New Edition. Crown 8vo. Cloth, price 6s.

Harold. A Drama. Crown 8vo. Cloth, price 6s.

Selections from Tennyson's Works. Super royal 16mo. Cloth, price 3s. 6d. Cloth gilt extra, price 4s.

Songs from Tennyson's Works. Super royal 16mo. Cloth extra, price 3s. 6d.
Also a cheap edition. 16mo. Cloth, price 2s. 6d.

Idylls of the King, and other Poems. Illustrated by Julia Margaret Cameron. 2 vols. Folio Half-bound morocco, cloth sides, price £6 6s. each.

Tennyson for the Young and for Recitation. Specially arranged. Fcap. 8vo. Price 1s. 6d.

Tennyson Birthday Book. Edited by Emily Shakespear. 32mo. Cloth limp, 2s.; cloth extra, 3s.

THOMAS (Moy).
A Fight for Life. With Frontispiece. Crown 8vo. Cloth, price 3s. 6d.

THOMPSON (Alice C.).
Preludes. A Volume of Poems. Illustrated by Elizabeth Thompson (Painter of "The Roll Call"). 8vo. Cloth, price 7s. 6d.

THOMPSON (Rev. A. S.).
Home Words for Wanderers. A Volume of Sermons. Crown 8vo. Cloth, price 6s.

Thoughts in Verse.
Small Crown 8vo. Cloth, price 1s. 6d.

THRING (Rev. Godfrey), B.A.
Hymns and Sacred Lyrics. Fcap. 8vo. Cloth, price 5s.

TODD (Herbert), M.A.
Arvan ; or, The Story of the Sword. A Poem. Crown 8vo. Cloth, price 7s. 6d.

TODHUNTER (Dr. J.)
Laurella; and other Poems. Crown 8vo. Cloth, price 6s. 6d.

TRAHERNE (Mrs. A.).
The Romantic Annals of a Naval Family. A New and Cheaper Edition. Crown 8vo. Cloth, price 5s.

TREMENHEERE (Lieut.-Gen. C. W.)
Missions in India : the System of Education in Government and Mission Schools contrasted. Demy 8vo. Sewed, price 2s.

TURNER (Rev. C. Tennyson).
Sonnets, Lyrics, and Translations. Crown 8vo. Cloth, price 4s. 6d.

TYNDALL (John), L.L.D., F.R.S.
The Forms of Water in Clouds and Rivers, Ice and Glaciers. With Twenty-five Illustrations. Seventh Edition. Crown 8vo. Cloth, price 5s.
Volume I. of The International Scientific Series.

VAMBERY (Prof. A.).
Bokhara : Its History and Conquest. Second Edition. Demy 8vo. Cloth, price 18s.

VAN BENEDEN (Mons.).
Animal Parasites and Messmates. With 83 Illustrations. Second Edition. Cloth, price 5s.
Volume XIX. of The International Scientific Series.

VINCENT (Capt. C. E. H.).
Elementary Military Geography, Reconnoitring, and Sketching. Compiled for Non-Commissioned Officers and Soldiers of all Arms. Square crown 8vo. Cloth, price 2s. 6d.

VOGEL (Dr. Hermann).
The Chemical effects of Light and Photography, in their application to Art, Science, and Industry. The translation thoroughly revised. With 100 Illustrations, including some beautiful specimens of Photography. Third Edition. Crown 8vo. Cloth, price 5s.
Volume XV. of The International Scientific Series.

VYNER (Lady Mary).
Every day a Portion. Adapted from the Bible and the Prayer Book, for the Private Devotions of those living in Widowhood. Collected and edited by Lady Mary Vyner. Square crown 8vo. Cloth extra, price 5s.

WARTENSLEBEN (Count H. von).
The Operations of the South Army in January and February, 1871. Compiled from the Official War Documents of the Head-quarters of the Southern Army. Translated by Colonel C. H. von Wright. With Maps. Demy 8vo. Cloth, price 6s.

The Operations of the First Army under Gen. von Manteuffel. Translated by Colonel C. H. von Wright. Uniform with the above. Demy 8vo. Cloth, price 9s.

WATERFIELD, W.
Hymns for Holy Days and Seasons. 32mo. Cloth, price 1s. 6d.

WAY (A.), M.A.
The Odes of Horace Literally Translated in Metre. Fcap. 8vo. Cloth, price 2s.

WELLS (Capt. John C.), R.N.
Spitzbergen—The Gateway to the Polynia; or, A Voyage to Spitzbergen. With numerous Illustrations by Whymper and others, and Map. New and Cheaper Edition. Demy 8vo. Cloth, price 6s.

WETMORE (W. S.).
Commercial Telegraphic Code. Second Edition. Post 4to. Boards, price 42s.

WHITAKER (Florence).
Christy's Inheritance. A London Story. Illustrated. Royal 16mo. Cloth, price 1s. 6d.

WHITE (A. D.), LL.D.
Warfare of Science. With Prefatory Note by Professor Tyndall. Second Edition. Crown 8vo. Cloth, price 3s. 6d.

WHITE (Capt. F. B. P.).
The Substantive Seniority Army List—Majors and Captains. 8vo. Sewed, price 2s. 6d.

WHITNEY (Prof. W. D.)
The Life and Growth of Language. Second Edition. Crown 8vo. Cloth, price 5s. *Copyright Edition.*

Volume XVI. of The International Scientific Series.

Essentials of English Grammar for the Use of Schools. Crown 8vo. Cloth, price 3s. 6d.

WHITTLE (J. L.), A.M.
Catholicism and the Vatican. With a Narrative of the Old Catholic Congress at Munich. Second Edition. Crown 8vo. Cloth, price 4s. 6d.

WICKHAM (Capt. E. H., R.A.)
Influence of Firearms upon Tactics: Historical and Critical Investigations. By an OFFICER OF SUPERIOR RANK (in the German Army). Translated by Captain E. H. Wickham, R.A. Demy 8vo. Cloth, price 7s. 6d.

WILBERFORCE (H. W.).
The Church and the Empires. Historical Periods. Preceded by a Memoir of the Author by John Henry Newman, D.D. of the Oratory. With Portrait. Post 8vo. Cloth, price 10s. 6d.

WILKINSON (T. L.).
Short Lectures on the Land Laws. Delivered before the Working Men's College. Crown 8vo. Limp Cloth, price 2s.

WILLIAMS (A. Lukyn).
Famines in India; their Causes and Possible Prevention. The Essay for the Le Bas Prize, 1875. Demy 8vo. Cloth, price 5s.

WILLIAMS (Charles), one of the Special Correspondents attached to the Staff of Ghazi Ahmed Mouktar Pasha.

The Armenian Campaign : Diary of the Campaign of 1877 in Armenia and Koordistan. With Two Special Maps. Large post 8vo. Cloth, price 10s. 6d.

WILLIAMS (Rowland), D.D.

Life and Letters of, with Extracts from his Note-Books. Edited by Mrs. Rowland Williams. With a Photographic Portrait. 2 vols. Large post 8vo. Cloth, price 24s.

Psalms, Litanies, Counsels and Collects for Devout Persons. Edited by his Widow. New and Popular Edition. Crown 8vo. Cloth, price 3s. 6d.

WILLIS (R., M.D.)

Servetus and Calvin : a Study of an Important Epoch in the Early History of the Reformation. 8vo. Cloth, price 16s.

WILLOUGHBY (The Hon. Mrs.).

On the North Wind— Thistledown. A Volume of Poems. Elegantly bound. Small crown 8vo. Cloth, price 7s. 6d.

WILSON (H. Schütz).

Studies and Romances. Crown 8vo. Cloth, price 7s. 6d.

WILSON (Lieut.-Col. C. T.).

James the Second and the Duke of Berwick. Demy 8vo. Cloth, price 12s. 6d.

WINTERBOTHAM (Rev. R.), M.A., B.Sc.

Sermons and Expositions. Crown 8vo. Cloth, price 7s. 6d.

WOINOVITS (Capt. I.).

Austrian Cavalry Exercise. Translated by Captain W. S. Cooke. Crown 8vo. Cloth, price 7s.

WOOD (C. F.).

A Yachting Cruise in the South Seas. With Six Photographic Illustrations. Demy 8vo. Cloth, price 7s. 6d.

WRIGHT (Rev. David), M.A.

Waiting for the Light, and other Sermons. Crown 8vo. Cloth, price 6s.

WYLD (R. S.), F.R.S.E.

The Physics and the Philosophy of the Senses ; or, The Mental and the Physical in their Mutual Relation. Illustrated by several Plates. Demy 8vo. Cloth, price 16s.

YONGE (C. D.).

History of the English Revolution of 1688. Crown 8vo. Cloth, price 6s.

YOUMANS (Eliza A.).

An Essay on the Culture of the Observing Powers of Children, especially in connection with the Study of Botany. Edited, with Notes and a Supplement, by Joseph Payne, F.C.P., Author of " Lectures on the Science and Art of Education," &c. Crown 8vo. Cloth, price 2s. 6d.

First Book of Botany. Designed to Cultivate the Observing Powers of Children. With 300 Engravings. New and Enlarged Edition. Crown 8vo. Cloth, price 5s.

YOUMANS (Edward L.), M.D.

A Class Book of Chemistry, on the Basis of the New System. With 200 Illustrations. Crown 8vo. Cloth, price 5s.

ZIMMERN (H.).

Stories in Precious Stones. With Six Illustrations. Third Edition. Crown 8vo. Cloth, price 5s.

THE NINETEENTH CENTURY.

A Monthly Review, edited by JAMES KNOWLES, *price* 2s. 6d.

Vols. 1 and 2 (Price 14s. each) and Vol. 3 (Price 17s.) contain Contributions by the following Writers:

The Duke of Argyll.
Mr. Matthew Arnold.
Rabbi Hermann Adler.
Mr. Arthur Arnold.
Rev. J. Baldwin Brown.
Mr. Edgar Bowring.
Mr. Thomas Brassey, M.P.
Mr. Edgar A. Bowring.
Sir Thomas Bazley, Bart., M.P.
Professor George von Bunsen.
Rev. Dr. George Percy Badger.
Rev. Canon Barry.
Dr. H. Charlton Bastian.
Professor Clifford.
Dr. Carpenter.
Professor Colvin.
Mr. Grant Duff, M.P.
Mr. Edward Dicey.
Rev. R. W. Dale.
Mr. J. A. Froude.
Mr. Archibald Forbes.
Rt. Hon. W. E. Gladstone, M.P.
Bishop of Gloucester and Bristol.
Mr. W. R. Greg.
Professor Huxley.
Mr. Frederick Harrison.
Mr. George Jacob Holyoake.
Mr. R. H. Hutton.
Mr. Henry Irving.
Sir John Lubbock, M.P.
Cardinal Manning.

Rev. Dr. Martineau.
Rev. Malcolm MacColl.
Professor Henry Morley.
His Highness Midhat Pasha.
Professor Henry Morley.
Mr. A. H. Mackonochie.
Rt. Hon. Lyon Playfair, M.P.
Mr. George Potter.
Viscount Stratford de Redcliffe.
Professor Croom Robertson.
Rev. J. Guiness Rogers.
Professor Ruskin.
Mr. W. R. S. Ralston.
The Very Rev. the Dean of St. Paul's.
Lord Selborne.
Sir James Fitzjames Stephen.
Rt. Hon. James Stansfeld, M.P.
Mr. James Spedding.
Professor Godwin Smith.
Professor Tyndall.
Mr. Tennyson.
Sir Julius Vogel.
Dr. Ward.
Major Gen. Sir Garnet Wolseley.
The Very Rev. the Dean of Westminster.
The Right Rev. Chas. Wordsworth, Bishop of St. Andrew's.
Mr. Frederick Wedmore.
Sir Thomas Watson.
&c. &c.

LONDON:
C. KEGAN PAUL AND CO.,
1, PATERNOSTER SQUARE.

CHISWICK PRESS:—CHARLES WHITTINGHAM, TOOKS COURT, CHANCERY LANE.

www.ingramcontent.com/pod-product-compliance
Lightning Source LLC
Chambersburg PA
CBHW021826230426
43669CB00008B/882